THE ORIGINS AND EVOLUTION OF THE SINGLE MARKET IN EUROPE

The Origins and Evolution of the Single Market in Europe

BILL LUCARELLI

Routledge
Taylor & Francis Group

LONDON AND NEW YORK

First published 1999 by Ashgate Publishing

Reissued 2018 by Routledge
2 Park Square, Milton Park, Abingdon, Oxon, OX14 4RN
711 Third Avenue, New York, NY I 0017, USA

Routledge is an imprint of the Taylor & Francis Group, an informa business

Notice:
Product or corporate names may be trademarks or registered trademarks, and are used only for identification and explanation without intent to infringe.

Publisher's Note
The publisher has gone to great lengths to ensure the quality of this reprint but points out that some imperfections in the original copies may be apparent.

Disclaimer
The publisher has made every effort to trace copyright holders and welcomes correspondence from those they have been unable to contact.

A Library of Congress record exists under LC control number: 99072654

ISBN 13: 978-1-138-33637-7 (hbk)
ISBN 13: 978-0-429-44304-6 (ebk)

Contents

List of Tables

List of Figures

Acknowledgments

This study would not have been possible without the diligent assistance of my two PhD Supervisors, Dr J. Halevi and Mr L. Haddad. To the former I am indebted to his numerous insights into the subject, his encouragement and constructive criticism. To the latter, I have appreciated his assistance in the technical aspects of the thesis and his critical comments.

I should also express my gratitude to the Political Economy Group at the University of Sydney for providing the academic space to research this topic. A critique of the prevailing neo-classical economic paradigm would not have been possible without their support and assistance.

List of Abbreviations

AGIP	Azienda Generale Italiana Petroli
BIS	Bank for International Settlements
CAP	Common Agricultural Policy
CEEC	Committee of European Economic Co-operation
CET	Common External Tariff
CIFE	Committee for a Federated Europe
COREPER	Committee of Permanent Representatives
DI	Divergence Indicator
DM	Deutsche Mark
EAGGF	European Agricultural Guidance and Guarantee Fund
EC	European Community
ECA	European Co-operation Administration
ECB	European Central Bank
ECSC	European Coal and Steel Community
ECU	European Currency Unit
EDC	European Defense Community
EEC	European Economic Community
EFTA	European Free Trade Association
EMFC	European Monetary Co-operation Fund
EMI	European Monetary Institute
EMS	European Monetary System
EMU	European Monetary Union
ENI	Ente Nazionale Indrocarburi
EP	European Parliament
EPC	European Political Co-operation
EPU	European Payments Union
ERM	Exchange Rate Mechanism
ERP	European Recovery Programme
ESCB	European system of Central Banks
ESPRIT	European Strategic Programme for Research in Information Technology
ETUC	European Trade Union Association
EU	European Union
FDI	Foreign Direct Investment

GATT	General Agreement on Tariffs and Trade
GDP	Gross Domestic Product
GNP	Gross National Product
IAR	International Authority for the Ruhr
IMF	International Monetary Fund
IMP	Integrated Mediterranean Programme
IRI	Instituto per la Riconstruzione Industriale
IT	Information Technology
MCA	Monetary Compensation Amount
MDS	Maximum Divergence Threshold
MEP	European Member of Parliament
MFE	European Federalist Movement
MITI	Ministry of International Trade and Industry
MNC	Multinational Corporation
NATO	North Atlantic Treaty Organisation
OCA	Optimum Currency Area
OECD	Organisation of Economic Co-operation and Development
OEEC	Organisation of European Economic Co-operation
OPEC	Organisation of Petroleum Exporting Countries
PPP	Purchasing Power Parity
RACE	Research and Development in Advanced Communications Technology for Europe
SCA	Semi-Conductor Agreement
SDR	Special Drawing Rights
SEA	Single European Act
TNC	Transnational Corporation
VSTF	Very Short-Term Financing Facility

Introduction

Objectivity in history - if we are still to use the conventional term - cannot be objectivity of fact, but only of relation, of the relation between fact and interpretation, between past, present and future (Carr, 1981, p.120).

As the title doubtless suggests, this study explores the development of the process of economic and political integration in Europe since the Second World War. The study intends to be a critique of the prevailing theories of negative integration which have informed the architects of European unification. According to these theories, the process of integration involves a gradual transfer of national sovereignty over the economic and political instruments of state power to an emergent supranational regime of governance. Negative integration implies that the process of economic integration should prefigure political union. The whole process is ostensibly governed by the dynamic of economic "spill-over". In other words, as strategic sectors of the national economy come under the auspices of supranational institutions, the logic of cumulative causation will impel Member States to relinquish their national sovereignty over other related sectors of the economy. It is possible to identify the formation of the European Coal and Steel Community (ECSC) in 1952 as the classical archetype of this process of negative integration. The success of the ECSC provided the institutional foundations of the Common Market which was enshrined by the signing of the Rome Treaties in 1958. In retrospect, the birth of the Common Market appeared to have vindicated the proponents of negative integration; the customs union would, it was assumed, eventually culminate in European federalism through the remorseless logic of economic and political "spill-over". According to a leading theorist of negative integration:

Spill-over does not require that all governments, groups and parties favour a given step for the same reasons; it requires only that a convergence of interests exists, concrete and extensive enough to enable a coalition to be constructed and powerful enough to make opponents of the general goal reluctant to bring about its frustration (pp.201-202)....Integration is rooted in interest, in the perception of the actors that they can better satisfy their aspirations in this new framework.....An ever widening circle of actors finds

1

> this system to be an effective, logical and appropriate framework in which to pursue its goals and this is one essential feature of a community (Lindberg, 1963, p.293).

The convergence of economic interests, however, might be undermined by competing national and class interests. In this case, the logic of negative integration appears to operate in reverse. The emergence of inter-state rivalries might in fact further strengthen the forces tending toward integration. National governments might perceive the benefits of expanding the role of supranational institutions in order to resolve these conflicts. This argument doubtless evokes certain liberal overtones in which the State is conceived as essentially autonomous and independent of class interests. State forms of mediation are thus necessary in a civil society governed by competing individual self-interest. An identical argument can be invoked to legitimise the existence of supranational institutions in order to reconcile competing national interests.

> The dynamics of spill-over are dependent upon the fact that support for any given step in integration is the result of a convergence of goals and expectations. These often competing goals give rise to competing activities and demands, which may be the basis for further convergence leading to further integration....Lack of agreement between governments may lead to an expanded role to the central institutions; in other words, Member States may delegate difficult problems.....Participation in a customs union will probably elicit reaction from non-member states, a situation that may create problems that can be resolved only by further integration or by expanding the role of central institutions (Lindberg, 1963, pp.10-11).

As national economies and sectors become more interdependent, the role of supranational institutions will tend to expand into the sphere of "high politics". Not only will national regimes of economic management and regulation be supplanted by supranational forms but the legislative and executive powers of national States over foreign and defense policies will eventually come under the auspices of supranational institutions. This evolutionary process will culminate in the federation of European nation-states and the birth of European statehood. In order to achieve this ultimate objective, a dynamic and entrepreneurial leadership is assigned to these supranational agencies. Unlike the federalist schema which proposes political unification as the precondition of economic integration, negative integration involves a functionalist strategy which views political union as the consummation of a long period of economic construction. Political union would signify the crowning of the edifice; the final act in the process of territorial enlargement and economic convergence.

Underlying the process of economic "spill-over" is the internal liberalisation of national barriers to trade, capital flows and labour mobility. The whole process is informed by neo-liberal economic doctrines which stress the economic virtues of national deregulation, the liberalisation of intra-European trade and the promotion of greater labour mobility across national frontiers but within an enlarged European "social space". After the creation of a customs union, the second stage of economic integration will involve closer macro-economic co-ordination between the national economies and the realisation of complete monetary union. Monetary union thus represents the highest stage in the construction of this economic edifice. A single currency would symbolise that economic convergence has now reached a stage in which political unification is possible.

In stark contrast to this idealised account of the schema of negative integration, there is a considerable body of literature that is critical about the methodological limitations of this form of economic determinism and the interpretation of post-war European history. These critiques basically challenge the national/supranational dichotomy by stressing the re-assertion of the nation-state in post-war European history. Quite contrary to pan-European interpretations, the emergence of supranational forms of mediation were essentially governed by the imperatives of national accumulation strategies. One of the most persuasive of these critiques is Milward's thesis that the Community represented a European rescue of the nation-state.

> The historical evidence shows that the real argument has never been about whether it is desirable that a supranational Europe should supersede the nation-state, but about whether the state can find a political and economic base for survival. The surrenders of national sovereignty after 1950 were one aspect of the successful re-assertion of the nation-state as the basic organisational entity of Europe. The Community was the European rescue of the nation-state. Since all history is change, that rescue could only be temporary and the process of economic development itself has eroded the political consensus which sustained both nation and supranation after the war (Milward, 1992, p.437).

In between these two divergent interpretations, there is a whole plethora of literature which often reflects an *a priori* bias either in favour or opposed to the ideology of European federalism. The argument proposed by this thesis is quite sympathetic to the ideals of European federalism.

Indeed, federalism is generally viewed as a progressive movement which contributed to the economic prosperity and peace of post-war European history. The theory of negative integration, however, fails to provide an adequate theoretical framework by which to interpret the origins and evolution of the European single market.

This thesis proposes that essentially two dominant tendencies have governed the whole trajectory of European economic integration. First and foremost, European integration constitutes a political/institutional process. Its most enduring feature has been the Franco-German axis which, in varying degrees, still provides the central pivot around which the intra-Community bargaining process revolves. Quite contrary to the theories of negative integration, the nation-state has prevailed with only a residual loss of sovereignty. At the very heart of this post-war settlement was the desire of European leaders - recruited mainly from the Christian Democratic parties - to avoid the possible re-emergence of destructive inter-state rivalry and establish a more liberal economic order in the wake of the disastrous experience of economic depression and war. In the aftermath of the Second World War, the imperatives of economic reconstruction and the realisation that economic survival was critically dependent on the cessation of inter-State rivalries had underpinned supra-national objectives. With the outbreak of Cold War rivalries, however, it was the intervention of American military and political power that ultimately provided the unifying rationale toward a pan-European project. At the very core of this problem was the future status of the newly emergent West German State.

In order to revive the European economy, it soon became evident that the German economy would provide the expansionary impetus through a dynamic symbiosis of trade and investment with the rest of Western Europe. In other words, the German economy would not only act as an engine of growth for the European economy as a whole, but would also provide an expanding market for European exports. The productive capacity of the West German economy was restored and harnessed within a supranational system of economic relations. After two failed attempts at territorial conquest and economic imperialism, the German economy would be restored as the economic powerhouse of Europe. In this sense, the historic causes of German expansionism, embodied in the issues of markets, investment outlets and access to strategic raw materials, could be resolved within a pan-European framework. At the same time, the perceived threat of a revival of German militarism could be contained by limiting the sovereignty of the West German State within the confines of European institutions.

The principal architects and arbiters of this post-war settlement were the Americans. American policy-makers were motivated by two overriding objectives. First, European economic reconstruction would provide markets and investment outlets for US capital and resolve the chronic trade imbalance across the Atlantic. Moreover, closer European integration based on liberal economic doctrines conformed with the post-war international economic order of *Pax Americana* which was enshrined in the GATT Agreements and the Bretton Woods Accords. The second strategic objective was primarily geo-political. With the onset of the Cold War, American statesmen supported the economic revival of Western Europe and Japan as strategic bulwarks in their "containment" policy against the perceived threat of Soviet and Chinese Communism.

In stark contrast to the prevailing theories of negative integration which interpret the evolution of the single European market as the product of an internal logic of economic cumulative causation, this thesis will stress the primacy of Europe's relationship with the United States and the pivotal role of Germany within Europe, as the *leitmotiv* in the process of integration. The making of Europe in the post-war era was essentially governed by American economic and strategic imperatives in the environment of Cold War politics. At the same time, the restoration of German economic power enmeshed the European economic sphere as an asymmetrical zone for the expansion of German exports and investment. The making of Europe was, in this crucial sense, the German answer to its own making.

The second dominant historical trend in the evolution of an organised European trading bloc has been the re-emergence of trans-Atlantic rivalry. This rivalry intensified with the onset of the international monetary crisis of the late 1960s and the ensuing economic slump of the early 1970s. European economic and monetary union appears to have been given further impetus in response to this phase of international economic crisis. With the breakdown of the fixed exchange rate system under the aegis of the Bretton Woods Agreements, the survival of the European project was imperilled by the onset of extreme exchange rate volatility and the spectre of competitive devaluations. European monetary union was catapulted to the forefront of the Community agenda with the publication of the Werner Report. Similarly, the threat posed by the penetration of US corporations in the European market had generated defensive impulses by European governments to counter the American challenge on a supranational level. By creating a larger, more unified internal market, European corporations could establish greater economies of scale and form strategic alliances to counter their more powerful American rivals.

The endogenous development of European capitalism since the war has been characterised by a peculiar dialectic between the imperatives of domestic accumulation mediated by the existing national States, on the one hand, and the objective necessity to furnish coherent supranational forms of State intervention and regulation in order to enlarge the territorial sphere of accumulation, on the other hand. This dialectic appears to be governed by both the historical terrain upon which European capitalism emerged after the war and by the logic of oligopolistic competition with their predominantly Japanese and American rivals in the global market.

From the standpoint of European capital, the national/supranational dichotomy has been an expression of the political conflict between European multinational firms which have pursued a neo-liberal strategy and the smaller national-based firms who have preserved a close dependency on their respective national States in order to protect their domestic markets. Yet this simple national/supranational dichotomy has also been complicated by the very limits imposed by the neo-liberal strategy which has failed to establish a parallel and dominant State apparatus on the supranational level. The crisis of European capitalism is at one and at the same time a political crisis of existing State forms of mediation and hegemony. Confronted by the incursions of international capital, European firms have adopted a defensive strategy by relying on their respective national States to provide a last line of resistance. German industrial capital appears to be the only exception insofar as their international competitiveness has not substantially diminished despite the maintenance of a relatively high nominal exchange rate. An analysis of the dynamics of European capitalism reveals that Germany has re-emerged to occupy the dominant, core position in the European economy. Its capital goods and manufactured exports enjoy an oligopolistic position which generate the accumulation of trade surpluses while the German mark has emerged as the nominal exchange rate anchor for the European monetary system.

This thesis will pose several theoretical issues which explicitly relate to the role of the State in the dynamics of capitalist accumulation. The post-war trend towards the growing globalisation of capital has had profound consequences for the existing hierarchy of nation-states and inter-State economic relations. In other words, how will the nation-state adapt and respond to the overwhelming demands of international capital? Indeed, will the nation-state continue to survive in its present form? More specifically, the issues of trade relations, investment and exchange rate policies will be highlighted to explore these tendencies. Given the limited scope of this study, it will not be possible to engage directly in this controversy. The intention will be to allude to these issues in the course of the historical narrative.

Since these theoretical issues still remain unresolved, it will be assumed that the nation-state continues to perform a strategic and structural role in the expanded reproduction of capital. The State will also be construed in the Gramscian sense of expressing hegemonic power in the mediation of capitalist social relations. It will be argued that instead of constituting an institutional obstacle to the globalisation of capital, the modern State has facilitated this process. This is reflected in the ascendancy of the neo-liberal paradigm in which the nation-state has provided a framework for the rise of the "informal empire of free enterprise" (Arrighi, 1978). The emergence of the Transnational Corporation (TNC) has circumvented traditional State mercantilist policies as intra-TNC trade has increased its share of the total volume of world trade. Similarly, the export of capital in the form of direct foreign investment (FDI) has increasingly superseded traditional trade flows through the export of commodities. Transnational corporations have demanded the abolition of State regulations and trade barriers which impede the movement of capital and trade across national borders. It will be proposed in this thesis that a neo-liberal strategy has governed the Internal Market Programme since the mid-1980s.

One of the central aims of this study is to analyse the dynamics of capitalist accumulation on a European scale and provide an alternative explanation to the prevailing theories of negative integration. Although the scope of the topic might appear quite ambitious from an empirical standpoint, the essential aim will be to construct a very broad historical narrative. In terms of periodisation, three distinct phases can be identified: (1) the formative period of post-war economic reconstruction between 1945 and 1955, (2) the phase of propulsive accumulation between 1955 and 1972, and (3) the phase of relative stagnation and crisis between 1972 and 1992. The basic outline of the study will be organised more or less around this historical periodisation.

In the course of the narrative, the thesis proposes several strategic questions: (1) what were the origins of the European project?, (2) what were the political and institutional dynamics that governed this process of economic integration?, (3) to what extent have international politico-economic relations conditioned its historical evolution? and, (4) what appears to be the most likely outcome of this historic project? In Part One, the origins of the Common Market will be explored in terms of the post-war economic recovery programme sponsored by the Americans. US strategic and economic objectives will be discussed in the context of the inter-State configuration of political forces within Europe. The formation of the customs union and the emergence of trans-Atlantic rivalry will conclude this narrative. Part Two explores the issue of European monetary union in some detail to reveal the emergence of these trans-Atlantic rivalries and the rise of German economic dominance within Europe. The Internal Market Programme will be critically analysed in Part Three. This will take the form of a critique of the efficacy of the neo-liberal strategy. The ultimate question, of course, is whether this historic project will eventually lead to political union. Several scenarios and hypotheses will be discussed in the conclusion.

In terms of methodology, a historical narrative appears to lend itself to this type of theorising. Given the scope of the topic, a narrow economistic analysis would not be appropriate. It would be more accurate to suggest that economics cannot be studied in isolation from politics. Indeed, the primacy of politics has characterised the entire process of economic integration in Europe. In the final instance, however, economic relations determine the parameters and constraints by which these political forces express themselves. The intention of this study is not to re-write history but to critically re-interpret the conventional wisdom. Most of the literature on the process of European integration has uncritically assimilated the prevailing neo-liberal economic paradigm. This theoretical framework is simply inadequate on both heuristic and historical grounds. Quite apart from its inherent failure to exhibit any critical content, the whole methodology is based on a rather crude economic determinism. The role of historical agency and the relative autonomy of social and political forces is either ignored or subsumed as the product of an inert mass of economic relations. The liberal economic doctrines that inform the logic of negative integration represent an ahistorical abstraction which deny the crucial and strategic role of the State in economic life. Negative integration assumes that historical change is governed by a gradual, incremental motion and that the interests of historical classes and agents are essentially harmonious and, if not, at least reconcilable.

In contrast to these theoretical constructs, this study will focus on the exogenous forces which have conditioned the development of the European trading bloc. The relationship between Europe and the United States on the one hand, and the emergence of German economic dominance within Europe, on the other hand, constitute the two axes along which the processes of European union have evolved. Rather than an exclusively internal logic of integration, it will be argued that the historical origins and evolution of the single market have been primarily governed by international relations of economic and politico-military power. The internal contradictions generated between competing national/class interests within Europe will also be highlighted. These divergent and centrifugal forces could threaten the post-war political consensus that has governed the process of European union. In other words, can the centre withstand the asymmetrical and regional shocks generated by market liberalisation that the neo-liberal strategy, albeit unwittingly, is bound to unleash?

PART I
EARLY ORIGINS
AND EVOLUTION

1 The Restoration of European Capitalism

Introduction

The origins of the single market in Europe can be traced back to the early post-war years during the implementation of the American sponsored European Recovery Programme (ERP). From a purely geo-political standpoint, European economic integration was a creature of the Cold War. For European leaders at the time, economic co-operation was perceived as a necessary political means to prevent the possible "Balkanisation" of Western Europe in the wake of superpower rivalries. Despite the proliferation of influential federalist groups which had emerged from the Resistance movements throughout Europe, the real impetus for European economic and political union emanated from the United States. Quite simply, the imperatives of the ERP had demanded closer co-operation between European governments to resolve the issues of economic reconstruction. Similarly, the outbreak of the Cold War in 1947 which culminated in the division of Europe into western and eastern spheres of influence, made the task of reconstruction more urgent. It was in this historical context that the restoration of the West German economy and its political rehabilitation emerged as the central problem confronting the American architects of the recovery programme (Lipgens, 1982).

It became quite evident, as far as the Americans were concerned, that the pre-war system of competing autarchic blocs and economic nationalism could no longer be justified as the basis for the post-war economic order. For the US authorities, multilateralism and trade liberalisation were viewed as the guiding principles for the post-war international economic order. European economic integration would furnish the institutional framework to promote these objectives as well as providing markets and investment outlets for American firms. At the same time, the expansion of European markets would provide an outlet for the US economic surplus which had been accumulated during the war (Kolko, 1972).

From the very outset, therefore, European economic reconstruction was conceived by American economic planners as an essential precondition for the preservation of US prosperity and growth. The very real possibility of an economic depression in Europe would inevitably engulf the United States itself. Consequently, the restoration of European capitalism had become synonymous with the future growth of the European market. However, this did not imply the reconstitution of the pre-war regimes of economic autarchy, trade blocs, financial controls and other more benign forms of State intervention and regulation. The US authorities committed themselves to the reformation of European capitalism in conformity to their vision of free trade and market liberalisation (Ambrose, 1971). By reforming European capitalism, it was envisaged that American business could benefit by creating an outlet for their investment, a market for their exports and the acquisition of raw materials from the former European colonies (Emmanuel, 1972).

I. The Legacy of the Inter-War Crisis

The tragic experience of the inter-war crisis which had been characterised by the collapse of world trade, financial turmoil and a sudden curtailment of productive output and investment, had left an indelible imprint on the consciousness of the post-war political elite. According to J.M. Keynes, the causes to this economic malaise could be attributed, to a large degree, on the adverse repercussions of the peace settlement enshrined by the Treaty of Versailles (Keynes, 1920). Under the terms of this agreement, German financial reparations were estimated at about $33 billion. No attempt was made to either scale down these payments or link them to the economic capacity of the vanquished to service them. At the same time, the victors found themselves indebted to the United States which had provided them with loans during the war. As a result, a triangular debt pyramid emerged in which France and Britain imposed reparations on Germany in order to settle their debts with the US. The Americans could have directly settled their loan repayments with Germany but this was considered too much of a risk since there was a greater likelihood of Germany defaulting on its obligations than the Allies.

The legacy of the Versailles settlement was quite disastrous. Efforts to promote economic reconstruction were severely constrained by the shortage of foreign exchange and credit. The only alternative was an expansion of exports. Yet as each country sought to curtail imports and increase exports, a vicious circle developed in which the demand for foreign exchange earnings through exports induced a series of competitive devaluations. Successive devaluations might have promoted exports for one country but the "fallacy of composition" implied that each other European country curtailed their propensity to import. Competitive devaluations soon degenerated into trade wars which threatened the international system of trade and monetary relations. With the disintegration of the international monetary system, financial speculation caused widespread damage to productive output and employment.

After the First World War, successive US governments chose to disengage themselves from the economic crisis in Europe and retreated into a policy of isolation. As the largest creditor nation and possessing a considerable trade surplus, the US could have extended loans for reconstruction and allowed greater access for European exports. The maladjustment of international balances of payments during the inter-war years merely accentuated the drift toward economic autarchy. The policy of isolation, however, proved to be ultimately self-defeating. This became glaringly evident with the collapse of the structure of debt that had been amassed during the 1920s. As J.M. Keynes had perceptively observed, the crux of the matter could be identified with the inability of Germany to earn export income in order to pay their reparations (Keynes, 1920). Denied access to their traditional export markets, Germany became highly dependent on US loans (ie, the Dawes and Young Plans) to temporarily resolve their chronic budgetary and balance of payments problems. Between 1924 and 1930 German governments had borrowed about 28 billion marks of which 10.3 billion were allocated to the payment of reparations (Aldcroft, 1978, p.62). Quite clearly this situation could not be sustained. It was the stock market crash of 1929 that exposed the basic weakness of Germany's financial position as US loans were terminated (Galbraith, 1981). Although the most indebted country, Germany's plight was not unique. Most of continental Europe, most notably the eastern European countries, were faced with balance of payments crises and financial indebtedness. A "depressive spiral" was set in motion as each country was impelled to adopt quite severe deflationist policies accompanied by an assault on the level of real wages which only worsened unemployment and the under-utilisation of productive capacity. In the course of this severe economic slump, bankruptcies and loan defaults multiplied.

As the demand for primary exports was curtailed after the phase of post-war reconstruction, an overproduction crisis developed in these sectors. The collapse in agricultural and raw material prices caused a general contraction in the volume of world trade which only further increased the severity of the financial crisis as the deterioration in the terms of trade of these primary producing countries hastened a series of loan defaults. After the stock market crash of 1929, a scramble for liquidity ensued in which US investors recalled their funds from abroad. This action merely triggered a vicious cycle of protectionist "beggar-thy-neighbour" policies as the indebted countries of Europe and the primary producing countries sought to protect their own domestic markets. A cumulative process of severe deflation, accompanied by a sudden collapse in income and output, characterised this depressive spiral as each country imposed import restrictions and capital controls. The outbreak of this "tariff mania" after the Hawley-Smoot Tariff enacted by the US authorities in 1930, culminated in the emergence of protectionist trading blocs and the ascendancy of national autarchic policies. In the words of H.W. Arndt:

> The combined effect of the fall in world prices, the contraction of international trade, the recall of short-term funds and the failure of continued American long-term investment brought about financial and economic crises in almost every country and in most of them set going cumulative processes of decline similar to that which was going on in the USA. The worst hit were the overseas primary producing countries which were brought to the verge of bankruptcy by the fall in agricultural and commodity prices, and the European debtor states, whose economic prosperity had been built up on continued foreign borrowing. Pressure on its gold and foreign exchange reserves forced one country after another to protect its currency by exchange rate depreciation or exchange control. At the same time, the efforts of every country to maintain its exports and protect its balance of payments by imposing increasing tariffs and import restrictions still further diminished the flow of international trade and increased the difficulties of every other country. The American slump and depression cannot be said to have caused the world depression, but they upset the unstable economic equilibrium of the world and gave the impetus to a similar economic decline in other countries (Arndt, 1963, p.19).

The existence of the gold standard regime made it more difficult for deficit countries to adjust to these external shocks. Under this regime it was not possible, in theory at least, for countries to adjust their respective exchange rates in the event of a capital flight or an adverse terms of trade. Since the relative value of all currencies was kept stable in terms of the gold standard, any imbalances in their international payments could not be corrected by an adjustment in the exchange rate but had to be corrected by an adjustment of national price or income levels. In other words, the fixed exchange rate pegged to the gold standard, tended to impart a powerful deflationary tendency in the deficit countries. The whole edifice of the gold standard had been constructed on the foundations of a competitive market economy. In this regime, the price mechanism constituted the sole means of exchange rate adjustment. Before the First World War, the gold standard had functioned quite smoothly as the free convertibility of national currencies fostered a multilateral settlement of international payments. If a country incurred a trade deficit, it would automatically experience a deflationary adjustment and an outflow of gold reserves. Conversely, a trade surplus would attract an inflow of gold reserves and a rise in nominal incomes and prices (Tew, 1960).

After the First World War, however, this international trade and payments equilibrium had disappeared. The United States emerged as the principal creditor nation to replace Britain as the major international investor. Between 1919 and 1929, US long-term investment abroad increased by almost $9 billion, accounting for about two thirds of the international increase in investment and about one third of the total (Aldcroft, 1978, p.74). Despite the emergence of the United States as the principal creditor nation after the First World War, its status as a reserve currency nation and "central banker" for the international payments system did not evolve until after the Second World War with the signing of the Bretton Woods Agreements which established a fixed, though flexible exchange rate system based on gold/dollar convertibility. During the inter-war years, however, the decline of Britain and the gold standard had only accentuated the chronic instability in international monetary relations. The UK itself had become a net debtor country and could no longer act as the "central banker" for the international capitalist economy.

The inevitable breakdown of the gold standard in 1931-33 was caused by the acute disequilibrium in the international balances of payment which were themselves an expression of the underlying problem of indebtedness and the concomitant collapse in the volume of world trade highlighted in Table 1.1.

Table 1.1   The Volume of World Trade (billions in gold dollars), 1929-33

	1929	1930	1931	1932	1933
Imports	33.6	29.1	20.8	14.0	12.5
Exports	33.0	20.5	18.9	12.9	11.7

Exports and imports are not equal because of statistical discrepancies and other factors.

Source: Sternberg, 1947, p.47.

In the immediate aftermath of the stock market crash, an avalanche of highly mobile, short-term speculative capital contributed to the instability and volatility of exchange rates. National governments responded by imposing capital and exchange rate controls. Economic autarchy gave rise to the formation of currency blocs and detailed State intervention in trade and international payments. Planned and managed trade relations eventually superseded the former laissez-faire, gold standard regime. In central Europe, trade had acquired barter-like forms with the emergence of exclusive bilateral commodity agreements. The general drift towards economic autarchy only hastened the ascendancy of economic nationalism and its more extreme manifestation in the guise of fascism.

The collapse of the gold standard was the central event of the process. International trade was deprived of a universally accepted means of payment and took barter-like forms, subject to detailed state mediation. Economic competition between individuals and firms of different nationalities became a phenomenon wholly internal to political rivalry among their respective states - a rivalry which progressively rose until it overflowed into the Second World War (Arrighi, 1978, p.75).

II. Post-War Reconstruction

Even before the end of the Second World War, American economic planners had envisaged the dismantling of the British system of preferential trade and the convertibility of the sterling area. The US Treasury had stipulated under Section VII of the Lend-Lease Agreement that aid would be conditional on the British forgoing their commercial advantages which excluded American business in the sterling area (Maier, 1987, p.135). During the war itself, the US had increased its exports from about $3b to $15b, most of which was destined to the Commonwealth markets (de Cecco, 1979, p.54). Before the war, the sterling area had accounted for over one third of the volume of world trade; its international cartels had controlled more than half of the share of the international commodity markets. The depletion of US domestic reserves of strategic raw materials, especially those of crude oil, had compelled them to seek access to new sources. In this sense, access to Middle East oil which had previously been dominated by British-Dutch cartels, became one of their overriding aims. To be sure, the whole basis of European reconstruction would be highly dependent on the importation of relatively inexpensive oil as these economies shifted away from coal-based industries. Between 1946 and 1953, the big five American oil corporations increased their share of Middle East oil output from 31 per cent to 60 per cent compared to a fall in the relative share of the British-Dutch cartels from 66 per cent to 31 per cent over the same period (Kolko, 1972, p.63).

After the war, the UK was technically bankrupt. The war itself had exhausted its foreign exchange reserves, while Britain's exports were estimated at only 31 per cent of their pre-war level (Lipgens, 1982, p.158). This burgeoning trade deficit was accompanied by the liquidation of their overseas assets and investments which had represented something of the order of a quarter of their pre-war wealth. According to Barratt-Brown: "Colonial holdings of sterling rose in the ten years after 1945 from 12 per cent to 32 per cent of the total holdings. To put it another way, British debts to the colonies rose from 450 million pounds in 1945 to nearly 1,300 million pounds in 1957" (Barratt-Brown, 1970, p.302). From its status as the world's foremost creditor nation at the turn of the century, Britain had become the world's largest debtor country in 1945. In order to cover their balance of payments deficit, estimated at about 2,100 million pounds, the British Treasury had no real alternative but to seek a major loan from the Americans.

Given the weak and vulnerable position of the British negotiators, they were compelled to succumb to American demands for trade and investment access in former British markets and the full convertibility of the pound/sterling area. In return, the US authorities would agree to finance a loan of $3.75b. With the signing of the Anglo-American Financial Agreement in December 1945, the US granted credits of $4.4b to the British government to be repaid over a fifty year period at 2 per cent per annum from 1951. Although the terms of the agreement were quite generous, the US had effectively dismantled the preferential sterling trade bloc. In this crucial sense, the agreement was to shed considerable insights into the *modus operandi* of US policy in the reconstruction of the European economies. Financial aid would become conditional on the willingness of European governments to agree to American demands for trade and market liberalisation. Within the Roosevelt administration, the State Department had seized the political initiative in advocating a system of free trade and multilateralism as the basis for the post-war economic order (Ikenberry, 1992). This ideological ascendancy over the economic planners and the architects of the New Deal Programme, had gained powerful allies in Wall Street financial circles who saw themselves as the natural heirs to the City of London. The whole tenor of this neo-liberal strategy asserted itself in the economic doctrines which informed the institutions and economic agreements of *Pax Americana*; from the IMF Charter, the GATT Agreements and most notably in the European Recovery Programme (ERP).

The American authorities were determined to avoid what they perceived to have been the bitter lessons of the inter-war crisis. They recognised quite perceptively that German economic recovery would constitute the essential precondition for the restoration of Western European prosperity. Despite the damage inflicted by the allied powers during the war, the German economy continued to possess the vast majority of its industrial plants still intact. The central problem, therefore, was how to harness German industrial capacity in order to rebuild the European economy without, at the same time, provoking national rivalries and a resurgence of German militarism. During the Yalta Agreements, a nominal reparations figure of $20b was proposed, though it soon became apparent that the Americans were quite reluctant to impose too harsh a reparations burden on Germany. On the other hand, the State Department was quite conscious of the need to placate and re-assure the former German occupied countries that the economic recovery would not re-kindle German rearmament. If the US could dictate the terms by which German reconstruction could be launched, it could then determine the structural features of a more liberal restoration of European capitalism.

The evidence appears to suggest that the US authorities had assimilated some of the lessons of the inter-war crisis. Trade liberalisation and currency stability were the twin objectives of US policy. While the Bretton Woods Agreements would furnish an international means of payments presided over by the IMF, the GATT Agreements would promote a more liberal trading system. Although this institutional framework would foster a more efficient and coherent mechanism of trade and payments, it could not in itself ensure an expansion of trade and economic growth. To resort to a simple metaphor: US policy was like a character in search of a script. At the very core of this problem was the structural trade imbalance between the US and Europe. The US authorities had designated this imbalance as essentially a European problem of production and productivity (Maier, 1987). It was therefore necessary to improve European productivity in order to restore the trans-Atlantic trade balance. By so doing, the European market would eventually provide an expanding outlet for American exports.

Customs union theory had informed the American strategy of economic recovery in Europe. It was proposed that economic integration would promote market expansion and an improvement in productivity and output through increased economies of scale. Moreover, greater economies of scale would induce a more dynamic environment for the promotion of technical progress. These arguments were doubtless inspired by the historical experience of US federalism and the evolution of "Fordism" and mass production. The European markets were, by contrast, inhibited by their highly protected and regulated national economies. In other words, American economic planners sought to resolve their problems of domestic surplus capacity by exporting to a unified European market. An increase in the level of effective demand in Europe would stimulate American exports and counteract the inherent tendency of the US economy toward economic stagnation (Baran & Sweezy, 1975).

The same problem that had emerged after the First World War in Europe had re-appeared again in 1945; the problem of where to obtain foreign exchange revenue in order to finance imports required for economic reconstruction. As the European economies recovered, a dollar gap appeared which threatened to sabotage the recovery. By 1947, the trade imbalance across the Atlantic had become quite acute. The American trade surplus was estimated at about $10b while the European trade deficit stood at about $7.5b. Three quarters of the European deficit was accounted by its trade with the US (Lipgens, 1982, p.471). Paradoxically enough, it was in fact the lightning rapidity by which the war-torn economies had recovered that had induced a high demand for imports from the US and had provoked balances of payment crises in Europe. The inflationary forces generated by the recovery had evoked memories of the economic crisis after the First World War as European governments resorted to the imposition of deflationary policies. Indeed, there was a very real likelihood of a relapse into the depressive spiral of the inter-war years with the re-emergence of national protectionism. In order to prevent this possibility, the Truman administration launched the European Recovery Programme and its financial counterpart, the Marshall Plan.

Quite contrary to some rather idealistic accounts, Marshall aid was never conceived solely as a humanitarian gesture to alleviate Europe's social and economic distress. Instead, the imperatives of Marshall aid were quite coherent in terms of providing the necessary finance by which European countries could purchase American exports. The dollar "famine" which had emerged after the war had imposed quite severe constraints on the capacity of European governments to purchase US exports for reconstruction. The re-emergence of regulated trade patterns and bilateral agreements in Europe posed a serious obstacle to American exports and evoked fears across the Atlantic that the world economy could, once again, lurch into economic depression. Marshall aid was a crucial instrument by which the US government could subsidise their exports and promote the liberalisation of trade. It would augment the liberal vision embodied by the international institutions and agreements inscribed under the aegis of *Pax Americana*. In short, the US sought to recast Europe in its own image. To this end, it became a powerful advocate of European federalism.

> By creating a United States of Europe, America could restore the equilibrium in world trade missing since 1914. Without that equilibrium, the multinational world of trade and payments at which American policy had aimed was impossible. By promoting European recovery, Marshall aid was bringing nearer, it was argued, the possibility of a world-wide equilibrium and a genuinely multilateral system. Thus European integration, no matter how political the immediate motives for seeking to promote it, was intellectually assimilated into the mainstream of earlier American foreign policy and there briefly reigned a happy harmony between political desirability and the alleged economic advantages of integration (Milward, 1984, p.59).

At the London Conference in July 1947, the US established the Committee of European Economic Co-operation (CEEC) to promote greater European co-operation in the implementation of the ERP. The sixteen members of the CEEC were viewed by the Americans as an embryonic supranational organisation which would eventually give birth to

European political integration.[1] This grand vision, however, soon encountered the realities of European national politics. Although economic co-operation was fostered, it failed to assume federalist forms and remained confined to purely functional and technical spheres. Under the conditions stipulated by the provision of Marshall aid, the United States could not only dictate how the aid was to be spent but could exercise considerable political leverage over the policies of European governments. Marshall aid was also deployed as a political weapon to outmanoeuvre and isolate the popular left-wing political parties which had acquired positions of power in the first few years after the war. As Cold War tensions escalated, the US authorities actively supported and mobilised the conservative forces represented by the various Christian Democratic parties and their counterparts to oppose the pro-Soviet Communist parties. In many cases, these tactics also led to the rehabilitation of former members of the discredited Fascist regimes. The strategic aims of the US would therefore be determined by their ability to galvanise political support within Europe. By 1949, the Left was in retreat throughout Europe and the Christian Democratic alliances had gained the political ascendancy.

The US also established the European Co-operation Administration (ECA) to administer the provision of reconstruction aid. It soon became evident, however, that the orthodox financial theories that informed ECA policies would be inadequate and inconsistent with the imperatives of European economic recovery. ECA policies were to prefigure the type of economic panacea familiar to developing countries in later years in the guise of IMF stabilisation and structural adjustment programmes. Aid would be conditional on the recipient government's willingness to implement orthodox monetarist policies of balanced budgets, stable currencies and the imposition of deflationary policies which implied a fall in real wages and the curtailment of private consumption. The promotion of exports at the expense of the domestic market was therefore the ultimate aim of ECA policy. This strategy would prove to be counter-productive since it merely accentuated competitive devaluations and provoked intra-European trade friction.

The formation of the European Payments Union was, to a certain degree, a logical reaction against the deflationary impact of ECA policies. While the US attempted to encourage monetary union based on the dollar

---

1   The CEEC comprised Austria, France, Belgium, Denmark, Italy, Luxembourg, the Netherlands, Norway, Sweden, Switzerland, the United Kingdom, Ireland, Iceland, Greece, Turkey and Portugal.

as the principal means of payment, the EPU evolved as a complex intra-European bilateral arrangement which settled monthly accounts through the mechanism of the "unit of account" issued by the Bank for International Settlements (BIS). The EPU limited the volume of debt that each country could accumulate against another country denominated in either of their respective currencies. If the debt exceeded these limits, payments were to be made in either gold or hard currencies (US dollars or Swiss francs). Quite contrary to American designs, intra-European trade was fostered independently of the dollar zone before the full restoration of currency convertibility. Indeed, the EPU could have evolved into an international clearing union similar to the Keynesian "Bancor" model proposed during the negotiations which had preceded the Bretton Woods Agreements. In this analogy, the "unit of account" could have provided the institutional framework for the evolution of a single European currency. However, national sovereignty over exchange rate policies had precluded any likelihood of monetary union; a theme that was to re-emerge in later schemes to achieve a single currency. The EPU became only a temporary arrangement designed to promote intra-European trade during the period of reconstruction. In the meantime, the dollar shortage continued to act as a major obstacle to the recovery programme despite the infusion of Marshall aid.

Towards the end of 1948, the US economy experienced a severe recession. The deflationary policies imposed by the ERP had contributed to the slump by dampening the level of effective demand in Europe. It became quite evident that the infusion of Marshall aid had failed to alleviate the impending crisis of overproduction in the United States. By mid-1949, US production had fallen by 15 per cent and unemployment reached a post-war high of 6.6 per cent (Kolko, 1972, p.9). At the very moment when European exports to the American market were essential in order to earn scarce foreign exchange, the Truman administration imposed import restrictions. In stark contrast to their free trade rhetoric, the US authorities resorted to protectionist policies as soon as their domestic markets were threatened. With the onset of recession, the ERP itself was imperilled as the US Congress began to impose limits on the ERP's financial appropriations.

Despite the US government's attempts to foster the growth of private investment abroad, US capital exports continued to be predominantly public in the form of grants and loans. Indeed, between 1945 and 1948, only an estimated 15 per cent of capital exports originated from the private sector (Kolko, 1972, p.621). The outflow of capital in the form of Marshall aid accounted for 2.1 per cent of the United States GNP in 1948, 2.4 per cent in 1949 and only 1.4 per cent in 1950 (Milward, 1984, p.94). Between 1945 and 1955, US loans and financial aid to Western Europe was estimated at $25b (Postan, 1967, p.103). By 1950 the European recovery had been quite impressive; all of the OEEC countries had exceeded their pre-war levels of growth. The liberalisation of intra-European trade had fostered a spectacular increase in export growth as Table 1.2 demonstrates.

Table 1.2   An Index of the Growth of Western European Exports (1948 = 100)

	1938	1947	1949	1950	1951
Belgium/Luxembourg	110	81	108	123	149
France	125	87	108	123	149
West Germany	481	38	188	435	622
Italy	124	67	113	140	175
Netherlands	156	69	151	204	242
United Kingdom	73	79	110	127	129

Source: UN Economic Survey of Europe Since the War, Geneva, 1953, p.225.

The European economies, however, continued to experience large trade deficits with the United States. Pressure began to mount in 1949 for a series of devaluations in relation to the US dollar in order to re-establish a trans-Atlantic trade equilibrium and stimulate exports to the American market. As Table 1.3 illustrates, the quite savage devaluations of September 1949 had transformed the European economies into export platforms.

Table 1.3   European Currency Devaluations in Relation to the $US (September 1949) Percentage Change

United Kingdom	-30.5
Netherlands	-30.2
France	-21.8
West Germany	-20.6
Belgium/Luxembourg	-12.3
Italy	-8.0

Source: Milward, 1984, p.293.

Conclusion

It can be surmised that the early origins of the Common Market were the product of a complex configuration of historical forces. The most important factor can be identified as the role of American economic and geo-political strategy in Europe. Although one should not attribute American policy with the kind of coherence and vision that is so often depicted by *ex post facto* narratives, it should be stressed that the possible emergence of a major economic slump had informed American policy in Europe. The US architects of the recovery programme had assimilated some of the lessons of the inter-war crisis and promoted European union in order to prevent the re-emergence of economic nationalism and autarchy. Economic reconstruction and recovery in Europe had become synonymous with the preservation of American prosperity. At the same time, a reformed and more liberal international economic order would promote American exports and investment. In this sense, the ERP was viewed as a crucial means by which the trans-Atlantic trade balance could be restored. The other overriding American concern was essentially geo-political. The perceived threat of Soviet expansionism provided the rationale to restore European capitalism and thus establish a *cordon sanitaire*. As will be discussed in the next chapter, the role of Germany in this post-war division of Europe was paramount.

Despite the vision and humanitarian tenor of Marshall aid, its critical failure was that it did not resolve the trade imbalance and the dollar shortage. It would be more accurate to suggest that it was the rapid growth of intra-European trade which had created the conditions for the economic recovery and had insulated the continent from the adverse impact of the US recession in 1948-50. The dollar famine had temporarily induced the imposition of import controls and bilateral trade agreements between European countries. In order to avert the re-emergence of protectionist "beggar-thy-neighbour" policies, the recovery of the German economy was critical. Indeed, as early as 1950, about half of the increase in intra-European trade had been attributed to West German imports. This implied that the German economy would play a critical role in the dynamics of post-war growth. At the same time, the exigencies of post-war reconstruction demanded a supranational solution to the pre-war problems of markets, investment outlets and access to raw materials. Closer economic and political co-operation would constitute a provisional solution. The origins of the single market therefore sprang from this formative period of post-war economic history. Despite the failure of US policy to foster a "United States of Europe", the political and institutional foundations established during the ERP provided the basis for a new phase of capital accumulation on a European scale. It was within the framework of trade liberalisation and multilateralism established under the aegis of *Pax Americana* that European institutions could evolve. The alternative scenario might have involved a relapse into the destructive syndrome of economic nationalism and the possible "Balkanisation" of Western Europe.

2 The Politics of European Integration; 1945-58

Introduction

In this chapter, the political configuration which gave rise to the Common Market will be explored. In contrast to prevailing neo-liberal interpretations, it will be argued that the logic of integration was governed by the need to restore the primacy of the nation-state. The process of intra-Community economic liberalisation did not imply the demise of national politics but represented a European rescue of the nation-state (Milward, 1992). At the very centre of this political consensus was the process of Franco-German rapprochement. The specific forms that this type of supranational mediation has acquired is reflected in the limits imposed on these supranational institutions and procedures. An analysis of the structure and organisation of Community institutions tends to confirm this interpretation. This is most evident in the drastic curtailment of the legislative powers conferred on the European parliament and the highly elitist and exclusivist forms of political dialogue that have characterised these supranational apparatuses. In the final instance, the primacy of the nation-state was preserved in the very limited surrender of national sovereignty inscribed in the Rome Treaties.

The Rome Treaties, signed in March 1957, represented the culmination of the strategy of negative integration. One of the central assumptions of this strategy was that the process of integration should be accompanied by the liberalisation of intra-Community trade. Barriers to the free movement of capital, goods, services and labour would be gradually abolished. Instead of a free trade area, however, a European customs union would be established. The evidence appears to suggest that the French propensity toward *dirigisme* was instrumental in the final blueprint in favour of a customs union despite powerful opposition from German industrial and financial circles.

For the proponents of European union, the Rome Treaties embodied overwhelming proof of the dynamics of economic "spill-over". After the relative success of the European Coal and Steel Community (ECSC), the logic of negative integration appeared to have been irrevocably set in motion. The mythology that still pervades the early pioneers of the Common Market - Monnet, Schuman, Adenauer and Hallstein - has become imbued with the kind of mystification that one normally associates with Christian sainthood. This analogy is quite apt because it was from the Catholic Church and the Christian Democratic parties that the most ardent converts to the European cause were recruited (Mayne & Pinter, 1990). Indeed, it would not be too conspiratorial to suggest that the fervent anti-Communism of these conservative forces played a crucial role in the birth of the Common Market. In this sense, the original six Member States would constitute a *cordon sanitaire* in the containment of the perceived threat of Communism (Galtung, 1973).

I. The Early Federalist Movement

Amidst the war-ravaged ruins of a divided Europe there emerged a widespread sentiment that the legacy of untrammelled nationalism and rivalry should be replaced by the ideals of a united, federated Europe. A pan-European movement, personified by Count Coudenhove-Kalergi, had been quite active in propagating federalist ideology before the war which had briefly culminated in the ill-fated Stresseman-Briand pact between France and Germany in the late 1920s. During the war itself, Churchill had proposed economic and political union between France and Britain in order to oppose the German occupation. In fact, many of the leading members of the Resistance movements had been early advocates of European federalism and despite their isolation during the war, had reached similar conclusions about the political necessity to abolish the existing system of competing nation-states.

> In the very heart of the anti-Fascist conspiracy during the Resistance, in the prisons, concentration camps and in the underground groups, some individuals had come to the conclusion that a pure and simple restoration of national states would be an absurdity. The two world wars had been a consequence of a Europe divided into national states. To restore these states even with a democratic form of government, and leave them in possession of national prerogatives would mean an inevitable rebirth of political and economic nationalism, thus perpetuating the cause of international conflicts (Spinelli, 1972, p.55).

For many of these federalist groups, the ideals of European federalism were to be eventually translated onto the international arena and give birth to an international federation of nation-states. The political inspiration for these ideas sprang from quite diverse and eclectic sources. Some proponents elevated the models of the United States and Switzerland as possible prototypes while others attempted to rekindle the anarcho-syndicalist writings of Proudhon and Bakunin. The most influential voice for the federalist cause, however, emanated from the Christian Democratic parties and was reflected in the anti-Communist rhetoric of Pope Pius XII. Whatever the sources of inspiration, it was widely believed that a return to the pre-war order could not be tolerated; nationalism had ostensibly lost its appeal and legitimacy (Delzell, 1960).

In July 1943, Resistance leaders from eight occupied countries met clandestinely in Geneva to issue a manifesto urging the federal union of European States after the defeat of Fascism. The manifesto called for the surrender of national sovereignty over defence, foreign policy and trade to a democratically elected European government. A month later, the European Federalist Movement (MFE) was launched. During the Paris Conference in March 1945, the MFE established the Committee for a Federated Europe (CIFE) whose aim was to mobilise popular support. Accompanied by a plethora of other more disparate federalist groups, the movement attracted considerable popular support. This populism, however, failed to generate any real opposition to the re-emergence and restoration of the post-war European nation-states. While the Christian Democratic and Social Democratic parties were sympathetic and accommodating to these federalist aspirations, the pro-Soviet Communist parties remained hostile and suspicious. Soviet leaders regarded European federalism as an anti-Soviet bloc designed to legitimise the Cold War division of Europe. After the failure of the federalist movement to generate any lasting impact on the post-war peace settlement, ideological divisions emerged within the movement, though these divisions reflected differences over strategy and means rather than ends (Swann,1978).

According to Spinelli, three different strategies for the new post-war political organisation of Europe can be identified: the federalist, the functionalist and the confederalist schemas. In the federalist approach, of which Spinelli was one of its main architects, it was envisaged that political unification and direct elections for a European Assembly would constitute the essential precondition for eventual economic union:

The federalists ask that the political institutions of a democratic Europe be constructed first, taking certain powers of initiative, deliberation, decision and execution from the national executives, parliaments and judiciary. The institutions would derive their legitimacy from the consent directly expressed by European citizens without interference from the Member States in matters of federal competence. Their models are like Switzerland and the great United States (Spinelli, 1966, p.11).

The functionalists, on the other hand, advocated a more gradualist strategy which had envisaged the formation of supranational administrative regimes that would foster co-operation between nation-states and through the cumulative logic of a "spill-over" effect would eventually lead to the surrender of national sovereignty over specific sectors of economic management. In other words, as national governments agreed to relinquish specific administrative agencies and policies to a supranational organisation, a cumulative logic would be set in motion which would expand the sphere of supranational prerogatives over other sectors. After the relative success of the European Coal and Steel Community, the functionalist strategy gained the political ascendancy. It was the pooling of coal and steel resources which led to the creation of parallel political forms of co-operation expressed by the formation of the High Authority. The pioneers of this approach were drawn largely from the Christian Democratic parties; their early practitioners were Monnet, Schuman, Adenauer and de Gasperi. Finally, the confederalist strategy stressed the primacy of the nation-state and viewed supranationalism merely in terms of inter-governmental co-operation. Early exponents of this approach were personified by Churchill and de Gaulle.

The apogee of the European movement culminated in the Congress of Europe which was convened by Churchill at the Hague in May 1948. The conference was attended by over eight hundred leaders in all spheres of public life and led to the creation of the Council of Europe which was inaugurated in Strasbourg in early 1949 under the chairmanship of Walter Hallstein. The Council comprised a Committee of Ministers and a Consultative Assembly represented by national delegations. Devoid of any real legislative powers, however, the Council eventually withered away and with it, the immediate aspirations of European federalists.

II. Franco-German Rapprochement

The real impetus toward closer European economic and political integration was to emerge from the process of Franco-German rapprochement. At the very centre of this process was the future role and status of the industrially strategic Ruhr region. With the onset of the Cold War, the Americans urged the rapid reconstruction of the German economy as a defence against the perceived threat of Soviet expansionism. It was also in West Germany that the US authorities could impose their neo-liberal policies without encountering widespread political opposition. These preoccupations were reflected in the fact that West Germany was the largest recipient of US aid, estimated at 28 per cent of the total in Europe. After successfully opposing French demands for the partition of the Ruhr, the Americans promoted Bizonia as a dollar zone and sponsored the creation of the West German republic in 1949. The coal-producing region of the Saarland, however, was still attached to France's economy, even though it had been granted a certain degree of political autonomy. It soon became evident that Germany's division would require a new trading system in Europe because of the loss of agricultural territories in the east. Consequently, the merger of the western zones would involve a European framework of trade to resolve West Germany's agricultural shortages. In order to reconstruct the West German economy, French co-operation was essential. At the very least, the dismantling of industry in the western zones by the French would have to cease. The West German authorities doubtless welcomed American support. Chancellor Adenauer had been perceptive enough to realise that US financial and political support would lend credence to West Germany's process of political rehabilitation and enable them to participate on a more equitable basis in the evolution of European supranationalism. The Americans therefore performed the role of mediator for West German interests by easing the burden of war reparations, sponsoring the re-birth of liberal democracy and, more importantly, by contributing to the restoration of West German industrial capacity (Reich, 1990).

American policy in West Germany encountered strident opposition and intransigence from France. Foremost in French concerns was their desire to ensure that their national security would not be imperilled once again by the possible resurgence of German militarism. Indeed, the enunciation of the "French thesis" by de Gaulle had sought to advance traditional geo-political ambitions over German territory in order to restore France to the status of a "great power" (Lipgens, 1982, p.213). According to this thesis, de Gaulle had supported the annexation of the German-speaking Saarland, international control over the industrial Ruhr region with a substantial share of its output directed toward French demands and the political break-up of Germany into separate States (Willis, 1968, p.31). In the face of Allied opposition, the French thesis proved to be untenable while de Gaulle's intransigence contributed to his resignation in January, 1946. By September 1949, the French zone of occupation was economically merged with the Bizone. After abandoning their policy of partition, the French authorities sought a common European jurisdiction over the region which provided the initial blueprint for the Schuman Plan. The economic requirements of the Monnet Plan had assumed access to the coal and coke resources of the Ruhr and Saarland (Kitzinger, 1961, p.20). The Schuman Plan was therefore formulated as a political response to the imperatives of the Monnet Plan which had guided France's economic reconstruction. Indeed, the Schuman Plan eventually rescued the Monnet Plan. French policies over the German question were ultimately driven by the imperatives of post-war reconstruction and tempered by security considerations.

The election of the first Bundestag of the German Federal Republic in August 1949 provided the unifying logic to post-war economic reconstruction. After the currency reform of 1948, the foundations of the West German economy were established. By October 1949, the Federal Republic had joined the OEEC and the newly established Committee that would preside over the creation of the ECSC. With the signing of the Petersburg Protocol with the Allies in November 1949, German national sovereignty was restored and the dismantling of German plants and equipment was terminated. The issue of French occupation of the Saarland, however, continued to act as a thorn in Franco-German relations. It became increasingly apparent that the demands of post-war reconstruction in both France and Germany would be dependent on their ability to acquire access to the coal and steel resources of the Ruhr region. In France, the Monnet Plan for economic reconstruction was threatened by a shortage of high quality coal and coke. Whereas France had exported a high proportion of their iron ore but only a relatively small amount to Germany, coal and steel exports had comprised a high level of German exports. The pooling of coal, iron ore and steel was therefore a rational trade-off in the French and German reconstruction plans. France would acquire access to the coal and coke resources of the Ruhr while Germany would increase its steel exports to France. At the same time, rationalisation and improved economies of scale could be achieved in these industries. The creation of a coal and steel cartel would promote more efficient and modern plants and mines as well as safeguarding producers and consumers from the vagaries of extreme price fluctuations.

Politically, the French authorities had sensed that it would be more opportune to determine the outcome of the ECSC while the nascent German State was still weak rather than after it had re-emerged as a major industrial power. Moreover, France could secure some control over these war-making industries and to paraphrase Schuman, to make war between the two countries "not only unthinkable but materially impossible" (Taber, 1974, pp.1-2). After a series of negotiations, Schuman and Adenauer officially announced the Franco-German Agreement in May 1950 which established a High Authority whose principal task would be to pool French and German production of coal and steel. Italy, Belgium, Luxembourg and the Netherlands were invited to participate. The final Paris Treaty which established the ECSC was signed by the six Member States in April 1951 and after national parliamentary ratifications, was legally in force in July 1952. The High Authority was given the difficult task of modernising and rationalising production, the harmonisation of freight rates and the abolition of national customs duties. If the ECSC proved to be successful, it would provide a blueprint by which other forms of sectoral integration could be fostered. Under the Paris Treaty this blueprint involved the creation of a European Assembly and a Court of Justice to preside over the ECSC. The Treaty of Paris thus prefigured the basic architecture of the Rome Treaties (Appendix A). In other words, it appeared to conform to the functionalist strategy of negative integration (Yondorf, 1965).

From the standpoint of Germany, the ECSC provided a means by which to restore some control over their basic industries from the allied occupation. The coal surpluses in 1949-50 had created a favourable climate for the negotiations over the ECSC but with the outbreak of the Korean War in 1951, an energy shortage emerged. Germany was forced to import coal from the United States at about twice the cost of their domestic production (Willis, 1968, p.113). Before the signing of the Paris Treaty, the International Authority for the Ruhr (IAR) which represented the allied occupation forces, was in control of most of Germany's coal and steel production. German resentment over the continued allied occupation increased as coal shortages developed in 1951. It was this political impasse that hastened German support for the Schuman Plan. The ECSC was, in the final analysis, a *fait accompli* imposed on Germany and viewed by the allies as a diplomatic gesture of Germany's willingness to participate in a pan-European framework (Henderson, 1962, p.131).

One of the primary objectives of the ECSC was the decartelisation of German industry. Endorsed by the earlier Potsdam Agreement, this policy sought to break-up the large trusts or *konzerne* who had exhibited close connections with the former Nazi regime. Despite energetic French efforts to implement this policy, progress was glacial and intractable. Although the I.G. Farben and Krupp cartels were systematically dissolved and property was confiscated by the Allied powers, the process of decartelisation of the German economy failed to make any real progress (Reich, 1990). By 1954, 24 separate companies were created in the steel industry and 23 in the coal industry (Willis, 1968, p.120). However, the three large banks which had dominated the German economy (the Deutsche, Dresdner and Commerz banks) remained intact, while most of the industrial cartels had either re-emerged or assumed new identities and ownership. One of the reasons for this failure was the US desire to restore German industrial capacity in order establish a an anti-Soviet bulwark in the Cold War division of Europe. The outbreak of the Korean War in June 1950 only intensified these US strategic imperatives. The US Secretary of State, Dean Acheson, went as far as demanding the rearmament of Germany which doubtless caused widespread opposition throughout Europe. Proposals for a European Defense Community (EDC) were inevitably defeated in the French Assembly in August 1954 (de la Mahotiere, 1968).

III. The Rome Treaties

Most explanations of the Rome Treaties highlight the expansion of intra-EEC trade as the *sine qua non* in the formation of a customs union (Hallstein, 1972, Hodges,1982, Swann, 1978, et al). Although this explanation is quite valid, it should be stressed that the role of Germany in this trade agreement was pivotal. The underlying rationale of the Rome treaties was governed by the need to become less dependent on American investment. It was assumed that a larger market would increase the level of productivity through greater economies of scale and contribute to an improvement in the competitiveness of European exports. Unlike the ECSC which had been governed by a regime of "regulated competition", the Rome Treaties were primarily informed by liberal economic doctrines.

The central pillar of the Rome treaties was the creation of a customs union through the progressive removal of quantitative restrictions to intra-European trade and the gradual liberalisation of capital markets. The formation of the Common Market would involve several conditions: (1) the free movement of capital, labour, goods and services across national frontiers, (2) the elimination of both tariff and non-tariff barriers to intra-Community trade and (3) the gradual harmonisation of fiscal and monetary policies and European technical standards and norms. Its Charter does not explicitly state the objectives of full economic union but is limited to the pursuit of trade and economic liberalisation within the confines of the Common External Tariff (CET). The Treaty does not recommend the creation of a single currency nor does it eliminate entirely differences in national fiscal, monetary and exchange rate policies. It can be surmised that the document is governed by the strategy of negative integration which is best illustrated in Article 2 of the Treaty:

> It shall be the aim of the Community, by establishing a Common Market and progressively approximating the economic policies of Member States, to promote throughout the Community a harmonious development of economic activities, a continuous and balanced expansion, an increased stability, an accelerated rise in standards of living and closer relations between its Member States.

Preliminary negotiations for the Treaties were initiated at the Conference of Messina in June 1955 by the Foreign Ministers of the six ECSC States. At this meeting, an inter-governmental Committee - chaired by the Belgium Foreign Minister, Spaak - was established to explore the most appropriate means by which to form a customs union. The creation of the ill-fated European Nuclear Energy Authority (Euratom) was also on the agenda. The Committee's report was presented in April 1956 and formed the basis for the political negotiations that preceded the formal ratification of the Rome Treaties. After a series of national parliamentary ratifications, the new institutions of the European Economic Community (EEC) and Euratom were officially inaugurated in Brussels on January 1st, 1958.

In contrast to the prevailing neo-liberal theories which had informed the strategy of negative integration, the original Spaak Report had been relatively interventionist (Holland, 1975). The authors had been influenced by the indicative planning methods of the French technocracy and had advocated a more interventionist strategy aimed at alleviating the structural and regional disparities which would have become more acute if a solely neo-liberal programme were to be implemented. In the absence of coherent and co-ordinated redistributive policies at the Community level, the impact of unfettered market forces would only accentuate these inequalities and have the perverse effect of undermining the process of harmonisation and economic integration. The economic theories which had informed the

Rome Treaties were, by contrast, informed by neo-liberal doctrines which stressed the ostensible virtues of competition, greater efficiency through specialisation and comparative advantage and the promotion of economies of scale to improve the level of productivity. Although economic planning was not entirely excluded as an instrument to militate regional and structural inequalities, the basic tenor of the Treaty was essentially neo-liberal.

One of the explanations for this ideological preference for a neo-liberal strategy can be identified with opposition to the Common Market within the ranks of the West German government and by the large German industrial conglomerates. A political clash had developed between Chancellor Adenauer who was ardently pro-European on the one hand and Erhard, the Economics Minister who had opposed the Common Market on the grounds that it would be detrimental to Germany's trading relations outside the customs union, on the other hand. German industrial and capital goods exports constituted about 88 per cent of its total exports. More than a quarter of these exports were destined to non-EEC Member States of Europe in the United Kingdom, Scandinavia, Austria and Switzerland (Willis, 1968, p.266). Supported by some of the most powerful economic interests in West Germany, Erhard proposed the creation of a more loosely organised free trade organisation which included the non-EEC members of Europe and the United States. Similarly, German industry held serious reservations about the French propensity toward *dirigisme* which would harm their trading interests. Given these German concerns, the final draft of the Rome Treaties acquired a more liberal form.

In retrospect, however, the expansion of German exports within the Common Market more than compensated for their loss of markets outside. West Germany emerged as the pivot around which European economic growth was re-launched. In this sense, the making of Europe represented the German answer to its own making. Germany accounted for 41 per cent of the EEC industrial output in 1957 compared to 28 per cent for France and 17 per cent for Italy, while its capital goods industry accounted for 55 per cent of the total (Taber, 1974, p.26). German capital goods exports made an enormous contribution to the technological reconversion and modernisation of European industry. At the same time, the dollar shortage had compelled European countries to switch their imports away from the US thereby favouring German exports. As Table 2.1 demonstrates, it was this dynamic symbiosis of trade interpenetration between West Germany and its EEC trading partners that characterised the propulsive phase of accumulation during the 1950s.

Table 2.1   Average annual percentage increase of the value of exports to (A) the Federal Republic and (B) the Rest of Western Europe, 1951-58

	(A)	(B)
Austria	21.3	6.7
Belgium/Denmark	13.8	1.8
France	16.2	2.6
Netherlands	12.6	7.7
Norway	12.7	2.7
Sweden	8.1	3.1
Switzerland	15.7	5.1
United Kingdom	13.9	3.5
Denmark	13.9	3.2

Source: Milward, 1992, p.137.

While West Germany's trade deficit with the dollar zone increased three fold between 1951 and 1957, its trade surplus with Western Europe increased by about three and a half times (Milward, 1992, p.166). West Germany therefore not only generated the impetus for Western European capital accumulation but also provided the largest market for industrial and agricultural exports from its Western European trading partners. Furthermore, exports to West Germany contributed to the stabilisation of Western European trade relations by partially insulating them from the frequent recurrence of US recessions.

Although West Germany emerged as the economic power-house of Europe this was not translated into political ascendancy. France performed the pre-eminent political role. One of the recurring themes of this study is that the EEC represented a European political consensus to prevent the re-emergence of German hegemonic ambitions. To this end, it was quite successful. As long as economic growth could be maintained, inter-State rivalry could be reconciled within a supranational framework. The other major historical development that imbedded this post-war political consensus was the geo-politics of the Cold War. Anti-Communism acted as the common bond that united these disparate national interests. A very brief summary of the institutions and the machinery of the Community is necessary to shed some insights into this inter-State bargaining process. A more detailed summary is given in Appendix B.

At the very apex of the hierarchy resides the Council of Ministers who are nominated to represent their respective national governments. The Council acts as the executive chamber whose decisions become Community law. Virtually all proposals for politically important legislation have to receive Council approval in order to be adopted. The Council is thus the supreme legislature vested with executive powers. The Commission, on the other hand, can be described as the legislative and bureaucratic agency which initiates proposals that are either accepted, rejected or modified by the Council of Ministers. The Commission also performs the crucial role of mediator by attempting to reconcile conflicting proposals and interests of Member States. Much of the policy-making machinery is channelled through a vast network of advisory committees. At the very epicentre of the Community decision-making process is the dialogue between the Commission and the Council. It is from this dialogue that regulations and directives are issued to the Member States. The European Court of Justice adjudicates the legality of Community legislation and interprets the general provisions of the Rome Treaty. This legal framework tends to distinguish the Community from other international organisations insofar as Community law can, in theory, override national laws.

In this overall schema, the European parliament merely performs a consultative function. Although it can impose a censure motion by a two thirds majority vote and dismiss the Commission, it cannot dismiss individual Commissioners nor can it appoint a new Commission. It is precisely the lack of legislative powers bestowed on the parliament that has been a perennial source of criticism and has reinforced widespread perceptions about the bureaucratic secrecy and Byzantine intrigues which permeate the politics of the Community. This "democratic deficit" has become a major obstacle to the cause of European federalism and is quite indicative of the primacy of national politics in the inter-Community bargaining process (Daltrop,1992, Deutsch, 1969, Hodges, 1982, et al). Although the relations of political power are an expression of shifting national alliances and the formation of power blocs, the prevailing functionalist view has been that the Commission has the scope and ability to act independently in order to pursue an expansion of the legislative powers of these supranational agencies. In the dynamic of political "spill-over", the Commission is assigned an entrepreneurial role (George, 1991). Contrary to these interpretations, the assumption of this study is that the scope for manoeuvre of the Commission is very limited. National imperatives appear to govern the political dynamics of the Community.

Although the Rome Treaties reflect the ascendancy of functionalist strategies over the federalist approach, it would be more accurate to contend that a confederalist regime has in fact evolved which is mirrored in the executive powers vested in the Council of Ministers. In this sense, Milward's contention that the EEC represented a European rescue of the nation-state appears to be quite plausible (Milward, 1992). This notion is borne out by the intricate machinery of consultation and mediation enshrined by the Rome Treaties to resolve competing national interests as well as by the "democratic deficit" of Community institutions and procedures.

Conclusion

Despite the emergence of popular and influential federalist movements, the nation-state was restored to its pre-eminent role in European political life. In this sense, it is plausible to suggest that the Community was the product of a political compromise over the issue of economic reconstruction. Post-war economic recovery demanded a supranational solution to the problems of markets, investment and access to strategic raw materials. The process of Franco-German rapprochement provided the political framework for the evolution of supranationalism. With the successful pooling of coal and steel resources, a functionalist logic of integration was set in motion which culminated in the formation of the Common Market. In retrospect, the proponents of negative integration appeared to have been vindicated. The Rome Treaties signified both a high point and the historical limitations of the functionalist strategy. Its very success was the harbinger of its eventual demise as the politics of nationalism, personified by France's General de Gaulle, re-emerged over the next decade.

Similarly, the post-war economic recovery and the rapid expansion of inter-Community trade provided the necessary conditions for the evolution of the Common Market. At the very core of this economic expansion was the recovery of the German economy which acted as both an engine of growth for the European economy and an expanding market for European exports. After two historic failures at conquest and territorial expansion this century, the immense productive forces of the German economy were rehabilitated and harnessed within a European framework. A recurring theme of this study is that the making of Europe represented the answer to Germany's own making. French concerns about the possible resurgence of German hegemonic ambitions could be allayed as long as a supranational framework could mediate and reconcile inter-State rivalries. In political terms, however, the primacy of the nation-state was preserved with only a partial surrender of national sovereignty. The EEC therefore represented a provisional solution to this national/supranational dichotomy. The historical significance of the Common Market was that it signalled a reversal of Europe's pre-war system of economic nationalism and inter-imperialist rivalry. American intervention and diplomacy played a central role in this post-war peace settlement. The American authorities were willing to tolerate a loss of markets in Europe in order to preserve the geopolitical imperatives of European political and military co-operation. In this crucial sense, the Common Market was a creature of the Cold War.

Appendix A

The Institutions of the ECSC

The High Authority

Originally comprised nine independent members who were appointed by a Council of Ministers. In order to ensure their political independence, the High Authority was granted the right to levy a one per cent tax on the annual coal and steel production of the ECSC.

The Council of Ministers

Appointed by the Member States of the ECSC, the Council had the power to veto the actions of the High Authority.

The Assembly

Appointed by the national parliaments of the six Member States, the Assembly could reject the High Authority's Annual Report by a two-thirds majority vote.

The Consultative Committees

These agencies were appointed by the Council of Ministers representing the producers, workers and consumer groups of the coal and steel industries.

The Court of Justice

The Court was established to interpret and adjudicate on the legal application of the Paris Treaty which enshrined the juridical framework of the ECSC.

Appendix B

The Institutions of the EEC

The Council of Ministers

The Treaty provides for three basic ways by which the Council can make a decision: (1) a qualified majority vote, (2) a simple majority vote and (3) unanimously. Unanimity is required for major decisions and new policy initiatives. A qualified majority vote is required for proposals designed to implement and amend existing legislation. Since 1992, France, Germany, Italy and the UK each have ten votes, Spain has eight, Belgium, Greece, the Netherlands and Portugal have five votes each and Luxembourg has two votes. Seventy per cent of the total votes (ie, 54 out of 76) constitutes a qualified majority. Under this system, the five larger countries cannot form a dominant minority. The simple majority vote is confined to minor procedural issues in which every Member State has one vote. The Council is advised by the Committee of Permanent Representatives (COREPER) who usually organise themselves into technical and ad hoc committees to study legislative proposals. Finally, the Presidency of the Council rotates every six months between the Member States.

The Commission

Situated in Brussels, the Commission originally consisted of nine members but after the three enlargements there are now seventeen Commissioners. Each of the five largest Member states (France, Germany, Italy, Spain and the UK) can appoint two Commissioners while the smaller seven countries have one representative each. A new Commission is appointed every four years but individual terms of office are renewable. The Commission elects a President every two years though this is usually extended to the normal four years of the Commission's term of office. Under Article 155 of the

Rome Treaty, the Commission is obliged to "formulate recommendations or deliver opinions on matters dealt with this Treaty, if it expressly so provides or if the Commission considers it necessary".

The European Parliament

Until 1979, European Members of Parliament (MEPs) were simply nominated by national parliaments. Since then, direct elections have been held every five years. With the exception of the UK, a uniform electoral system has been devised, though the legislative powers of the European Parliament remain limited. Although it can impose a censure motion by a two thirds majority vote and dismiss the Commission, it cannot dismiss individual Commissioners nor can it appoint a new Commission. The political and procedural reforms adopted by the Single European Act in 1985 gave the EP greater legislative powers to amend Council proposals. If the EP's amendments are accepted by the Commission, then the Council can only reject these amendments by a unanimous vote whereas only a majority vote is required by the Council to accept these amendments. Parliamentary approval is also required for the application of new membership to the Community.

The Court of Justice

The European Court has two overriding objectives: (1) it is responsible for the application and adjudication of Community law and (2) the interpretation of the general provisions of the Treaty. It comprises of fifteen judges, each of whom is appointed for a renewable six year term by their respective Member States. A President of the Court is elected for a three year term while eight Advocates-General are assigned individual cases.

The European Council

Although the Treaty did not make any provision for Summit meetings by the Heads of governments, informal meetings were held quite regularly and by 1974, these Summits acquired a more formal structure. Since then the European Council has included the President of the Commission and other members of the Commission as well as the respective Foreign Ministers of each Member State. These meetings have been convened to resolve difficult political issues and circumvent the bureaucratic immobilism of Community legislation.

The Economic and Social Committees

These Committees were originally appointed by the Council of Ministers for a four year term to advice them on social and economic issues. The membership is drawn mostly from employer associations, trades union and professional organisations. Specialist sub-committees are also formed to advice on technical matters in the formulation of policy and legislation.

3 The Formation of the Customs Union; 1958-72

Introduction

The evolution of European union has often been depicted by its proponents as a process involving three progressive stages. The formation of a customs union would inevitably prefigure complete economic union which would, in turn, set in motion the conditions for political union. The mechanism by which this process is ostensibly governed involves a gradual functionalist logic of cumulative causation. In this "snowball effect" there is an underlying assumption of economic reductionism. The relationship between economics and politics, however, is infinitely more complex than this simple schema might suggest. As E.H. Carr has quite succinctly observed: "The science of economics presupposes a given political order and cannot be profitably studied in isolation from politics" (Carr, 1951, p117). It was the re-entry of President de Gaulle on the European stage that exposed the basic fallacy of this functionalist logic. Indeed, the first decade of the customs union was dominated by the political crisis caused by de Gaulle's divergent vision of a confederated Europe constructed on the foundations of the nation-state. Inextricably linked to this political struggle were the issues of an independent Community budget, the Common Agricultural Policy (CAP), the future role of the European Parliament and the issue of Community enlargement with the application of British membership.

The Treaty of Rome had envisaged a period of twelve to fifteen years by which the removal of internal tariffs and quantitative restrictions would be gradually accomplished behind a common external tariff. Customs union theory had informed the architects of the Treaty that trade creation within the customs union would not only compensate but would exceed the potential economic losses incurred by the negative impact of trade diversion. In its classical formulation, Viner defines the "trade-diverting" and "trade-creating" effects of a customs union between two hypothetical countries as follows:

47

When the trade-creating force is predominant, one of the members at least must benefit, both may benefit, the two combined must have a net benefit, and the world at large benefits, but the outside world loses, in the short-run at least, and can gain in the long-run only as a result of the general diffusion of the increased prosperity of the customs union area. Where the trade diverting effect is predominant, one at least of the member countries is bound to be injured, both may be injured, the two combined will suffer a net injury, and there will be injury to the outside world and the world at large (Viner, 1950, p.44).

The process of completion would be accompanied by the introduction of qualified majority voting in the Council of Ministers and the creation of an independent Community budget financed largely from the revenue accrued from customs duties and levies. If progress in the political sphere was paralysed by de Gaulle's intransigence, the process of intra-Community trade liberalisation proved to be highly successful. An initial ten per cent reduction in the average level of intra Community industrial tariffs had already been implemented in 1958. Five years later, industrial tariffs were reduced by a half; a target that had exceeded the original thirty per cent envisaged by the Treaty of Rome.

The abolition of internal barriers to trade and investment had contributed to the expansion of intra-Community trade and to economic growth in general. In the first fifteen years of the customs union, intra-Community trade was estimated to have grown by an average annual rate of 15.1 per cent or had increased six-fold. By contrast, the annual average rate of growth in world trade was estimated at 8.4 per cent. By 1972, more than fifty per cent of Community trade was between Member States compared to about thirty per cent in 1958 (Taber, 1974, p.17). German economic recovery provided the engine of growth for Western Europe as a whole. A relatively undervalued Deutsche mark and an abundant labour supply (including the 2.5 million refugees from the east) generated the economic recovery (Bulmer & Paterson, 1987, p.56). A similar process occurred in the Community as a whole in which over five million workers migrated from the Mediterranean regions to the industrial centres of northern Europe (Aldcroft, 1978, p.166). In the wake of the Korean War boom, industrial production had increased by over forty per cent between 1953 and 1957, while intra-EEC trade had expanded by about 75 per cent over the same period (Krause, 1964, p.147). The rates of capital formation were very high during the 1950s. As a percentage of GDP, capital formation was estimated to have averaged 27 per cent per annum in West Germany, 20 per cent in France and 16 per cent in Italy (Maier, 1987, p.176). Quite clearly, the Common Market had generated improvements in the economies of scale, productivity and in the terms of trade with the emergence of the world's largest internal market. The dynamic of trade creation both reinforced and acted as a catalyst in the phase of post-war economic growth.

I. The Political Consequences of Gaullism

The Gaullist strategy of opposing federalist objectives on the one hand, while supporting the Common Agricultural Policy, on the other hand, was bound to be incompatible. Agricultural protectionism required a supranational framework. This implied a partial surrender of national sovereignty over agricultural trade policies. At the same time, de Gaulle's vision of a loose confederation of European nation-states and his strident insistence on the preservation of national sovereignty could no longer be reconciled with the realities of France's partnership with West Germany. France's aspirations for political leadership in Europe did not correspond with their relative economic power; a partnership with West Germany was essential.

> The objective of a "European Europe" was widely accepted in France. But for some time there had been growing concern among thoughtful Frenchmen at the glaring contradictions in de Gaulle's European policy. France needed partners, above all Germany, if she was to build a "European Europe"; yet de Gaulle seemed bent on alienating the Germans and driving them into even greater dependence on the US (Camps, 1967, pp.96-97).

Two related themes can be identified in the Gaullist European strategy. First, France pursued a foreign policy which opposed American hegemony in Europe and viewed the Community as a political mediator or "third force" in the polarisation of the Cold War. In this sense, de Gaulle sought closer diplomatic and economic relations with the Soviet Union while at the same time, France would develop its own military and nuclear capability. In this scheme, the United Kingdom was not considered a reliable European ally and a potential threat to French aspirations for political leadership in Europe. Furthermore, British ambivalence, if not antipathy, towards the CAP merely reinforced de Gaulle's veto on British entry into the Community in 1963 and 1967. The second strand of the Gaullist strategy was a contradictory mixture of French nationalism and the promotion of a "European Europe" which would preserve the primacy of the nation-state (Pinder, 1991, pp.11-12). In other words, de Gaulle was an indefatigable opponent of the federalist cause but was not entirely hostile to the European ideal as long as French interests could be promoted within this supranational framework.

The French position inevitably encountered opposition from the West German government whose economic interests favoured British entry into the Community. British membership would encourage the entry of the European Free Trade Association (EFTA) countries with whom a considerable share of German trade was conducted. Britain's more liberal trade policies also shared a close affinity with German ideological preferences. It soon became evident, however, that special trade concessions for the Commonwealth countries would complicate the existing arrangements for the CET. British membership was thus conditional on their willingness to terminate their preferential trade agreements with the Commonwealth. In retrospect, the legacy of Britain's failure to join the Common Market was quite damaging as they experienced a loss of markets in Europe. In order to mitigate their loss of market share in the EEC, the UK initiated negotiations with the six non-EEC members of Switzerland, Austria, Portugal, Sweden, Norway and Denmark to form the EFTA in July 1959. In an obvious challenge to the Common Market, the EFTA agreed to reduce tariffs on industrial goods by an average twenty per cent in July 1960 and to abolish all tariffs and quotas within ten years (Willis, 1968, p.283).

The EFTA was condemned to be overshadowed by Britain whose relative economic power and market size dwarfed the other countries. Similarly, the EFTA was not recognised by the EEC authorities who preferred to negotiate with each individual Member State. By negotiating the EFTA Agreements, the UK sought to preserve their trade relations with the Commonwealth and pursue their traditional policy of trade and commercial competition with the continental powers. If Britain had joined the Common Market it would have been forced to import more expensive agricultural goods and contribute financially to the CAP. Their traditional links with the Commonwealth, however, had ensured that they would benefit from the importation of less expensive primary goods and thereby improve their comparative advantages in terms of higher purchasing power parities and lower real wages (Evans, 1973). In political and diplomatic terms, the UK perceived its role as a mediator between Europe and America. British ambivalence, however, was viewed as a confirmation of their Anglophile, geo-political tactics of "divide and rule" by the continental countries (Nairn, 1971). The Gaullists had portrayed the British as the "trojan horse" of the Americans. Regardless of British intentions, the EFTA was never in a position to challenge the Common Market, given the comparative size of their internal market. Indeed, despite the existence of trade barriers, the continental members of the EFTA gravitated toward West Germany. The volume of trade between the EFTA and Germany had increased by 150 per cent between 1958 and 1969 (Hallstein, 1972, p.87).

Conflict over the financing of the Community budget and the formation of the CAP were to dominate the Community's political agenda in the first decade. From the very outset, de Gaulle had opposed proposals to establish an independent Community budget rather than relying on the financial contributions of Member States. The whole issue of political autonomy depended quite critically on the ability of the Community to furnish their own financial resources. Despite the benefits that would accrue to France with the financing of the CAP, de Gaulle continued to oppose Community "own resources" on the grounds that it would constitute a threat to national sovereignty over fiscal policies. At the same time, the rapid progress achieved in the liberalisation of intra-Community trade made it possible to introduce the CET in 1967, two years earlier than was originally planned. With the formation of the customs union, it was envisaged by the Rome Treaty (Article 205) that revenue accrued from the CET would provide the financial base for a Community budget. The Commission would be endowed with legislative powers to frame the budget while its adoption would be the prerogative of the Council of Ministers. This would coincide with the introduction of qualified majority voting in the Council. Monnet and earlier federalists had proposed that the Community should possess its own budget in order to prevent individual Member States from withdrawing their financial contributions and sabotaging Community resources. The issue of "own resources" was therefore closely interwoven with federalist aims. These federalist aims were, doubtless, anathema to de Gaulle's vision of Europe (Camps, 1967).

In order to persuade French officials to support Community proposals for "own resources", the Commission announced a "package deal" which would involve the completion of farm price negotiations, a Community budget financed by revenue through levies on agricultural imports and an increase in the European Parliament's legislative powers over the budget. French officials responded by demanding the resolution of agricultural finances independently of all other issues. This political impasse culminated in the withdrawal of French Ministers from the Council in July 1965 in what became known as the "empty chair" policy (Pinder, 1991). As a result, the Community was thrown into disarray. By January

1966 de Gaulle was obliged to abandon this policy in favour of a political compromise. After a series of negotiations, the principle of qualified majority voting in the Council was modified to apply only to technical rather than political issues. The famous "Luxembourg Compromise" re-affirmed France's right of veto in the Council while the issue of parliamentary powers over the budget was postponed. An "agreement to disagree" had in effect been reached. In retrospect, however, de Gaulle's victory proved to be rather pyrrhic. The issue of Community "own resources" remained suspended until de Gaulle's resignation in 1969. A Community budget was ratified by the Hague Treaty in April 1970 which signalled the completion of the customs union. By 1975, a Community budget financed largely from the levies and customs duties accrued from the CET and a one per cent value-added tax on goods and services was introduced. This process of "deepening" was accompanied by an enlargement of Community membership to include Britain, Denmark and Ireland in 1971 (Daltrop, 1992).

II. The Common Agricultural Policy

Post-war agriculture exhibited most of the characteristics of a declining sector; it had a low level of productivity, was uncompetitive in world markets and lacked an innovative dynamism. Its survival increasingly depended on State support. Although the CAP emerged as the largest Community project, accounting for 70-80 per cent of the Community budget, agricultural protectionism did not constitute the primary aim of the Rome Treaties. The customs union was primarily concerned about industrial trade between the Member States. The objectives of the CAP were enshrined in Article 39 of the Rome Treaty. These included the stability of markets and prices, an increase in agricultural efficiency and productivity by promoting technical progress, reasonable prices for consumers and an improved standard of living for agricultural producers. The Treaty provided for the gradual elimination of intra-Community barriers to agriculture over a twelve to fifteen year period to be replaced by a common agricultural tariff which would coincide with the implementation of the CET (Hine, 1985).

The politics of the CAP was closely enmeshed with French economic imperatives. By 1960 the French authorities came under increasing pressure to find markets for their mounting agricultural surpluses and to improve the income of their farm sector. Foreign, extra-Community competition could be countered with the formation of an agricultural common market. Within the Common Market itself, French producers encountered quite intense competition from Italy and the Netherlands. West Germany represented the largest and fastest growing market since most of their former agricultural territories in the east had vanished. Agricultural imports from the Netherlands and France had increased from 20 per cent in 1962 to about 38 per cent of the total in 1972 (Milward, 1992, p.315). Not only did West Germany emerge as the largest agricultural market but it also subsidised Community agriculture even though it could have imported less expensive primary goods from outside the Common Market.

One could quite easily contend from this observation that the CAP embodied a rational trade-off between French agricultural interests and West German industrial imperatives. Whereas the West Germans sought a common market for their industrial exports, the French pursued a similar policy for their more efficient agricultural exports. The West German authorities were thus quite willing to incur the financial burdens of the CAP in order to ensure a captive market for their industrial exports. This thesis, however, has been debunked by Milward who argues that the CAP was in fact solely a Franco-Dutch initiative to resolve their respective agricultural surpluses (Milward, 1992). The only other explanation lies in the fact that the CAP was essentially a political compromise to placate the powerful agricultural lobbies in Europe, including those in West Germany. Indeed, the survival of the Conservative and Christian Democratic alliances were critically dependent on these rural constituencies despite their relative decline in both economic and demographic terms. On economic grounds alone, the CAP could not be justified.

After reaching an agreement on the instrument of a variable import levy which would be necessary to establish a common price for each agricultural commodity, the implementation of the import levy became the subject of quite prolonged and intensive negotiations by the Six. While the Germans advocated a more liberal regime which would minimalise the level of protection and ease their financial burden, the French and the Dutch insisted on a more interventionist system of price support. In order to ensure a reasonable return to the producer, a target price was set for each commodity. If world prices fell below this target, the Agricultural Fund would be deployed to maintain price stability by purchasing surplus production. The CAP soon evolved into a complex web of regulations covering price targets for almost every agricultural commodity. By the end of 1963 more than three hundred of these regulations had been adopted by the Council covering grains, rice, poultry, eggs, pork, beef, dairy products, wine, fruit and vegetables. These commodities comprised about 85 per cent of the total agricultural output or about $20b (Lindberg, et al, 1970, p.147). National governments were still allowed to establish their own price support but within the agreed price range. Agreement over individual target prices was a slow and protracted process. Countries with high price levels such as Germany, Belgium and Italy had to lower their support levels and experience a relative fall in their agricultural income. Conversely, the more efficient producers such as France and the Netherlands were compelled to increase their price support which implied an increase in the cost of living but an improvement in the income of the farm sector.

By July 1964 the first Mansholt Plan was implemented with the agreement on common agricultural prices. Within two years the scope of the single market for agriculture was extended to include fats and oils, milk and dairy products, beef and veal, sugar and rice. In the following year (1967), the crucial target price for wheat was finalised which translated into an increase in the export of cereals by France to the Common Market from $32m in 1958 to $713.7m in 1971 (Taber, 1974, p.39). In July 1968 the CAP was officially inscribed in Community legislation which transferred agricultural policy under the auspices of Community decision-making. The European Agricultural Guidance and Guarantee Fund (EAGGF) was established to finance the cost of the CAP. While the Guarantee section finances price support, the Guidance section of the fund was formed to finance structural policy to improve agricultural productivity. The main emphasis, however, is on price support operations with only six per cent of EAGGF expenditure devoted to the Guidance section (Nugent, 1991, pp.347-48). After the initial phase of import protection, the Community was faced with ever increasing stockpiles of agricultural surpluses with which it began to dump at subsidised prices on world markets. Market support therefore shifted from a policy of import regulation to one of export subsidisation. It was this development which provoked retaliatory trade policies from the Americans and had escalated into a major trade war by the 1970s (Pinder & Pryce, 1969).

In December 1968 the second Mansholt Plan was presented to the Council as a blueprint for agricultural reform. It was proposed that over a ten year period support prices should be lowered and subsidies gradually curtailed in order to encourage a process of restructuring. The aim was to curtail employment in agriculture by about half. Agricultural productivity would be improved by increasing farm sizes and promoting greater mechanisation and rationalisation. The Community would provide grants and loans to promote investment, economies of scale and improvements in the basic infrastructure. Agricultural reform proved to be a difficult task. Although the number of people employed in agriculture gradually fell by about 2.6 million between 1968 and 1978, it failed to reach the projected target of about five million. Regardless of Community policies, the migration of labour to the urban centres was consistent with a long historical trend. Post-war economic growth had merely accelerated this trend. The size of farm holdings, however, remained relatively unchanged while the disparities between farm incomes had increased. At the same time, average farm income continued to decline in relation to non-farm income. These policies ultimately failed to militate against the mounting surplus capacities. Between 1974 and 1984, as a percentage of consumption, production of cereals grew from 91 to 116, output of meat from 96 to 101, butter from 95 to 134 and sugar from 95 to 134. Over the same period, agricultural exports from the Community increased by 256 per cent but imports by only 14 per cent (Pinder, 1991, p.85).

The crisis of overproduction in agriculture caused considerable disruption in world markets, while the growing stockpiles only increased the financial burden of maintaining the CAP which had accounted for about 80 per cent of the Community budget expenditure. Agricultural policies had become captive to powerful agricultural lobbies and political forces. The overall level of agricultural protection was in fact higher after the introduction of the CAP than under the former national regimes of protectionism (Milward, 1992, p.314). Its pivotal role in the inter-Community bargaining process not only influenced the development of political institutions but was reflected in the sphere of monetary policies. With the onset of the dollar crisis in the late 1960s, exchange rate volatility had the effect of destabilising agricultural prices and the price support regime of the CAP. In an effort to foster cohesion in intra-Community agricultural prices, "green" rates of exchange were introduced by the Agriculture Ministers to fix agricultural prices independently of the market rates of exchange. These green rates were expressed in units of account equal in value to the US dollar (Coffey & Presley, 1971). To ensure that divergences between market rates and green rates would not distort agricultural trade, a system of border levies and subsidies known as Monetary Compensation Amounts (MCAs) were also introduced. These measures, however, imposed a further drain on the Community's finances and failed to prevent distortions generated by extreme exchange rate fluctuations. It was precisely at this historical juncture that French and German interests converged over the issue of monetary integration with the publication of the Werner Report in 1972 (Coffey, 1977).

Although agriculture did not constitute a central component of the Kennedy Round of the GATT negotiations, it emerged as one of the most contentious issues in subsequent GATT Rounds. Indeed, agricultural trade had originally been excluded from the official GATT negotiations. Under Article 11 of the GATT Agreements, the United States had applied for exemption in agriculture as early as 1955 in order to protect their domestic producers. As a result, negotiations over agricultural trade could not be resolved until the Americans withdrew their waiver (Josling, 1989). Despite this stalemate over agricultural trade, the Kennedy Round made considerable progress in the liberalisation of industrial trade. Between 1964 and 1967, industrial tariffs in the OECD had been reduced by an average of about 30 per cent. Within the Common Market, progress was even more impressive; by July 1967, internal tariffs on industrial goods had been reduced by an average of sixty per cent since the ratification of the Rome Treaties in 1958 (Camps, 1965, p.46).

Conclusion

After the formation of the customs union, the Community emerged as the largest internal market and trading bloc in the world. With the exception of agriculture, the economic gains generated by the dynamic of trade creation had exceeded the potential losses accrued by the adverse impact of trade diversion. Furthermore, the sheer size and scale of the customs area had considerably improved the terms of trade of the Community in relation to the rest of the world. Viner's theorem in this sense appears to have been validated.

> The greater the economic area of the tariff-levying unit, the greater is likely to be, other things being equal, the improvement in the terms of trade with the outside area resulting from the tariff. A customs union, by increasing the extent of the territory which operates under a single tariff, thus tends to increase the efficacy of the tariff in improving the terms of trade of that area vis a vis the rest of the world...the level of foreign tariffs can be affected in some degree through tariff bargaining and the larger the bargaining unit, the more effective its bargaining can be (Viner, 1950, pp.55-56).

In the first decade of the customs union, intra-EEC trade had quadrupled and had increased by about twice the rate of the volume of world trade. By 1972, the Community had accounted for about forty per cent of international trade compared to about 18 per cent for the United

States. If one excludes intra-Community trade, the enlarged Community accounted for almost twenty per cent of the share of world trade (Taber, 1974, p.89). EEC exports to all non-member countries increased from $16.2b to $45.8b between 1958 and 1970, while total imports from non-member countries increased from $16.2b to about $45b over the same period (Bailey, 1973, pp.115-116). Translated into political and diplomatic terms, the CET and the Common Commercial Policy (Article 113 of the Rome Treaty) had imparted enormous bargaining power and leverage in trade negotiations.

Between 1958 and 1970, the growth of German trade inside the Common Market was estimated at 500 per cent, Italy's trade had grown by 933 and France's trade by 763 per cent (Hallstein, 1972, p.88). Table 31 summarises the annual rate of increase in intra-Community imports and exports between 1954 and 1972.

Table 3.1   Annual Average Percentage Increase in Intra-Community Trade; 1954-72 (Imports/Exports)

	1954-58	1959-65	1966-72
Total	11.7/11.7	17.1/17.1	15.7/15.7
Belgium/Luxembourg	9.5/9.6	13.2/16.4	14.8/14.4
France	15.0/9.8	18.8/20.5	17.5/16.4
Germany	15.2/13.2	19.9/15.9	15.6/15.3
Italy	5.6/14.8	20.2/25.2	19.7/15.2
Netherlands	11.6/11.6	14.9/15.1	12.3/16.0

Source: Taber, 1974, p.172.

A more accurate summary of the share of intra-Community imports and exports by each country is illustrated in Table 3.2.

**Table 3.2   Intra-Community Imports and Exports as a Percentage
of the Total; 1958-72 (Imports/Exports)**

	1958	1965	1972
EC Total	29.6/30.2	41.7/43.5	51.6/49.8
Belgium/Luxembourg	46.6/45.1	54.5/61.9	64.3/68.5
France	21.9/22.2	38.8/41.0	50.4/49.9
Germany	25.8/27.3	38.1/35.2	48.8/39.9
Italy	21.6/23.9	31.3/40.2	44.9/45.1
Netherlands	41.9/41.5	53.4/55.7	56.3/64.8

Source: Taber, 1974, p.172.

It should also be noted that the share of exports as a percentage of GDP in the original six Member States had increased from an average of 14 per cent to 19 per cent between 1958 and 1972. Over the next decade, this exports/GDP ratio increased to an average of 29 per cent by the enlarged Community (Brocker, et al, 1985, p.129). Much of this expansion of intra-Community trade reflected the rapid rate of economic growth generally. In the 1960s the rate of growth was estimated at 67 per cent in real terms which compared to 48 per cent for the US and about 30 per cent for the UK (Bailey, 1973, pp.115-116).

From the standpoint of political progress toward European union, the first fifteen years were characterised by relative immobilism and inertia. The institutional framework established by the Treaty of Rome lacked cohesion and was vulnerable to the re-assertion of the nation-state exemplified by the politics of de Gaulle. Gaullist opposition, however, merely postponed the development of Community institutions. This national/supranational dichotomy has continued to inform the provisional and enigmatic character of Community institutions and procedures. The gulf between the prerogatives of national sovereignty and federalist aspirations, embodied by the Luxembourg Compromise, appeared irreconcilable. For all practical purposes, the functionalist strategy was under a perennial state of siege. At the same time, the legacy of the CAP proved to be both economically irrational and politically untenable in terms of the diplomatic fall-out which emanated from agricultural producing countries.

4 The Emergence of Trans-Atlantic Rivalry

Introduction

Competition over markets and investment outlets between American corporations and their emergent rivals across the Atlantic became interwoven with inter-State rivalries. The rapid internationalisation of capital merely intensified these competitive forces. As American corporations increased their penetration of the European market, defensive impulses were generated by European nation-states to counter the American challenge. It was primarily from this development that the EEC evolved from an exclusively political bloc - in response to the demands of post-war reconstruction and the Cold War division of Europe - into an organised trading bloc. Quite contrary to neo-functionalist interpretations, the logic of integration was, to a large degree, driven by international competition and rivalry. Mandel's thesis appears to correspond with this crucial development:

> In this sense, one may say that the movement towards Western European economic integration via the Common Market is a product of capitalist penetration on an international scale: an attempt by capitalism to reconcile the level of productive forces and the degree of monopolistic concentration with the survival of the nation-state. By creating a larger area in which commodities, capital and labour circulate freely, it thereby releases industry from at least part of the fetters which Malthusian cartels, tariff walls and short-sighted economic nationalism had imposed upon it in the inter-war years (Mandel, 1975, p.143).

The emergence of trans-Atlantic rivalry during the 1960s was the culmination of two inter-related factors. First, the inflow of American direct investment in the Common Market evoked fears of the spectre of industrial colonisation (Servan-Schreiber, 1969). Second, the outflow of US dollars contributed to the deterioration of successive US current account deficits which ultimately undermined the stability of the US dollar as a means of international payments and reserve currency. Accompanied by the financial burden imposed by the maintenance of the global American military umbrella, the stability of the dollar and the international regime of fixed exchange rates could no longer be preserved. Indeed, it was in this pervasive international environment of exchange rate volatility and inflation during the dollar crisis of the late 1960s that convinced European political leaders of the necessity to create a zone of monetary stability. In this sense, the demise of the international monetary system under the aegis of the Bretton Woods Agreements, represented a decisive turning point in the development of the European trading bloc. An enlargement of the territorial space in order to satisfy the need for expanding markets and investment outlets by European transnational firms was perceived as a necessary and logical response to counter competition from their US rivals. The EEC therefore represented a possible solution to this problem of "territorial non-coincidence" (Murray, 1971). This strategy, however, encountered the limits of the traditional forms of capitalist regulation and intervention which were still organised on a predominantly national level.

I. The American Challenge

The initial outbreak of trans-Atlantic rivalry was triggered by an avalanche of US direct investment in Europe. Several explanations for this American strategy can be identified. Through the agency of the transnational corporation (TNC), the European market attracted direct foreign investment rather than exports from the United States because of the formation of the Common Market. In order to avoid the high trade barriers and the higher costs associated with an export strategy, American corporations established subsidiaries and industrial transplants inside the Common Market. The advantages offered by this strategy were evident by the larger economies of scale, technological superiority and greater financial resources at the disposal of US corporations over their European rivals. Surplus profits could be captured in the Common Market by adopting an oligopolistic strategy of market pre-emption to eliminate potential competitors. According to Vernon, US direct investment was governed by the product cycle in which the monopolistic advantages conferred by their ownership of technological innovations had generated demand for American exports. As these foreign markets are saturated and the innovations are diffused, however, overseas corporations lose their oligopolistic advantages. In order to prevent the loss of these foreign markets, oligopolistic competition compels TNCs to establish subsidiaries in close proximity to local markets (Vernon, 1966).

The other major explanation for the expansion of US direct investment abroad was the pre-eminent role performed by the dollar as the international means of payments and as the principal reserve currency which provided a coherent vehicle by which the profits of American corporations could be converted and re-invested in global capital markets. The restoration of currency convertibility in Europe in 1958 had induced an unprecedented inflow of US capital. Similarly, as a result of an overvalued US dollar, American corporations could purchase foreign assets more cheaply and could take advantage of relatively lower foreign wages. The security and stability of the gold/dollar regime not only provided a favourable environment for long-term investment but also allowed American firms to borrow on more attractive terms in international capital markets. The pre-eminent international status of the dollar therefore promoted the expansion of US direct investment abroad (Gilpin, 1975).

Although the trans-Atlantic trade balance was in relative equilibrium insofar as European exports to the American market had, more or less, compensated for the penetration of US exports in Europe, the value of US direct investment in Europe was estimated at two and a half times greater than European exports to the American market. More than 70 per cent of US investment in Europe took the form of direct investment while the European equivalent in the US was only about 30 per cent (Balassa, 1966, p.120). Most of this inflow of American investment was concentrated in the manufacturing and petro-chemical industries. European firms, by contrast, invested in portfolio holdings in the financial and services sectors of the US economy. The volume of American direct investment as well as the technological and financial advantages enjoyed by American corporations had provoked a defensive strategy of mergers and acquisitions in Western Europe in order to counter the American challenge (Mandel, 1970).

As has already been noted, the formation of the Common Market was instrumental in attracting American direct investment; between 1957 and 1967, the value of US direct investment in the Common Market had more than quadrupled (Tugendhat, 1971, p.45). The book value of US direct investment in the Common Market had increased from an estimated $2.1b in 1959, $11.8b in 1970 and reached $16.8b in 1972 (Franco, 1976, p.134). Before the Rome Treaties, the United Kingdom had been the major destination of US investment abroad which had, in turn, provided access to the Commonwealth markets. With the formation of the Common Market, however, American corporations embarked on a major investment drive to capture a share of this large expanding market. The emergence of these mass markets were ideal in exploiting economies of scale through the techniques of mass production and marketing. The rapid growth of US industrial transplants encouraged joint rationalisation of production between parent and subsidiaries through the standardisation of upstream operations and the creation of marketing, sales and service facilities. A high degree of linkage was thus possible between foreign firms and their locally based subsidiaries. The advantages of this kind of collaboration not only increased the opportunities for optimum production but also fostered the transfer and diffusion of new technologies and production techniques. The other major advantage enjoyed by American corporations was their greater access to internal financial resources in contrast to their European rivals who were more reliant on external sources of finance (Tugendhat, 1971).

Most of the inflow of US direct investment was concentrated in the more technologically advanced sectors of industry. In the computer industry, US subsidiaries and acquisitions of European firms had accounted for over 70 per cent of the European market in 1968 while in the automobile industry, the US share the market (including the UK), had increased from 20.9 per cent to 28.8 per cent between 1960 and 1969 (Hu, 1973, p.32). In 1967 it was estimated that 40 per cent of total US investment originated from only three corporations: Standard Oil, General Motors and Ford, while two thirds had been accounted by only twenty US corporations (Tugendhat, 1971, p.54). The impact of American competition was quite profound in terms of the transfer of new technologies and organisational techniques which contributed to an improvement in productivity and impelled their less productive European rivals to emulate the American "model". This growing technological gap was evident in the American expenditure on Research and Development which had exceeded Community spending by a factor of three (Vernon, 1971, p.90). Indeed, capital/labour ratios in the EEC were estimated at only 40 per cent of those in the US (Balassa, 1966, p.144). The European response to the American corporate invasion induced an unprecedented wave of mergers and acquisitions and fostered collaborative agreements on the Community level to promote R & D (ie, Airbus, Eurotom, etc).

The merger boom within the Community during the 1960s was, as a general rule, defensive rather than offensive. With few exceptions, European firms were much smaller than their US rivals and lacked the financial resources to either compete in their domestic markets or to establish subsidiaries in the American market. To be sure, the leading US manufacturing firms were on average twice as large as their European counterparts in terms of their ownership of assets (Servan-Schreiber, 1969). In response to the American challenge, European firms undertook a strategy to improve their internal economies of scale through programs of rationalisation and technological reconversion and upgrading. This necessarily implied an increase in the rate of mergers and acquisitions. According to the Colonna Report, the magnitude of this trend toward greater concentration of economic power during the 1960s is revealed in Table 4.1.

The most striking evidence from the Colonna Report was the relatively small number of intra-EEC mergers and take-overs. Indeed, most mergers and acquisitions had occurred in the same country while the rate of foreign ownership of European firms had peaked in 1967 which coincided with the completion of the customs union but declined thereafter. The fact that the rate of trans-European interpenetration of capital was relatively low suggests that the political structures of the EEC had not been developed to prevent hostile take-overs of European firms. Confronted by American competition, European firms resorted to their respective national governments to defend their economic interests. It can also be surmised that the export of commodities rather than FDI was the prevailing method of economic expansion by European firms. Intra-EEC trade in manufactured goods expanded by a factor of 3.2 between 1963 and 1971 (Franco, 1976, p.144). Instead of inducing the formation of trans-European corporations, the American corporate invasion merely intensified national rivalries within the EEC. This was evident in the opposition of the French government to the attempt by Italian car-maker, Fiat, to gain control of Citroën and the West German government's opposition to France's Compagnie Francaise des Petrole's bid to acquire a 30 per cent stake in Germany's Gelsenberg oil corporation. Quite apart from nationalistic policies, the existence of divergent legal, taxation and financial regimes on the national level continued to pose considerable obstacles to the formation of trans-European corporations.

Table 4.1　Mergers and Take-Overs (or controlling interest) in the EEC; 1961-68

	Same Member Country	Different Member Country	By a Member Country in a Third Country	By a Third Country in a Member Country
1961	131	19	26	102
1962	162	11	21	85
1963	157	28	9	82
1964	172	34	18	110
1965	228	17	20	70
1966	221	31	20	93
1967	253	32	36	115
1968	272	35	29	106
Total	1596	227	179	763

Source: Colonna Report, EEC Commission, 1970.

An analysis of the relationship between the dominant fractions of capital and the nation-state might shed some insights into the industrial structure and the political dynamics of Western European capitalism. Industrial firms in France and Italy were more vulnerable to the American corporate invasion. State intervention played a strategic role in fostering national mergers and defending "national champions". In Italy, State holding companies known as the *imprese a partecipazione statale* are essentially industrial conglomerates in which the State owns a controlling interest. These conglomerates dominate Italy's industrial anatomy. The largest and most strategic is the *Instituto per la Ricostruzione Industriale (IRI)* which controls most of the iron and steel industry, shipbuilding, communications, civil aviation and a substantial share of the engineering and construction industries. The other major State holding company is the *Ente Nazionale Indrocarburi (ENI)* which controls most of the oil refining, natural gas and petro-chemical enterprises. Within the energy sector, *Azienda Generale Italiana Petroli (AGIP)* has performed a strategic role in both the upstream and downstream production of petroleum and natural gas. The State also owns a major car manufacturer (Alfa Romeo) and the three largest commercial banks (Banca Commerciale Italia, Credito Italiano and Banca di Roma). Italy's leading private enterprises also enjoy a close relationship with the State sector. These include Montecatini-Edison in chemicals, Olivetti in electronics, Snia-Viscosa in artificial fibres, Fiat in automobiles and Pirelli in tyres. In 1966 Montecatini and Edison merged in response to the threat posed by the US chemical giants while Pirelli merged with Britain's Dunlop in 1970 to form the second largest tyre producer in the world.

In France, the role of the State in fostering mergers and acquisitions on the behalf of their national enterprises has also been quite extensive. The French have been enthusiastic exponents of *dirigisme*. In the steel sector, the French authorities pursued a strategy of encouraging greater rationalisation and increased economies of scale. In 1964 the De Wendel steelworks and Sidelor established a common subsidiary - Sacilor (Société Des Aciéries De Lorraine) - while the other steel producers, Unicor and Lorraine-Escaut, merged in 1966 and soon after acquired a controlling interest in the large steel firm, Vallourec. In the wake of these mergers, Unicor and Wendel-Sidelor controlled over two thirds of the steel output in France. In the automobile industry, Citroën launched a successful take-over of the small French auto-maker, Panhard, in 1965. Although Renault and Peugeot continued to operate as separate enterprises, closer collaboration was fostered between them by the French State in their research and development programs. In the aviation sector, Sud-Aviation was formed by a merger between Sud-Ouest and Sud-Est in 1965. A similar process of industrial concentration occurred in the electrical and electronic industries in which Compagnie Générale d'Electricité, through a series of take-overs, dominated the market in France (Lieberman, 1977).

The German State, by contrast, was less interventionist. Although State planning and regulation was quite pervasive during the formative years of post-war reconstruction, the German authorities adopted a more liberal economic strategy in the mid-1950s. The strident anti-inflationary stance of the Bundesbank has played a determinant role in the inherently anti-Keynesian policies of the German State. Economic liberalism, however, has not prevented the rapid growth of oligopolistic market power in the German economy. The high degree of economic concentration continues to be evident in the close links between the three largest banks (the Deutsche, Dresner and Commerzbank) and their cross-ownership and interlocking directorships with the most powerful industrial conglomerates (Edwards & Fischer, 1994). Whereas the four largest West German chemical firms (Hoechst, Bayer, BASF and Henkel) had accounted for 40 per cent of the national market in 1952, this share had increased to over 70 per cent in 1972. A similar trend occurred in the steel industry in which the four major producers (Hoesch AG, Thyssen, Krupp and Salzgitter) controlled 90 per cent of the national market in 1972 compared to 58 per cent ten years earlier. In the car industry, Volkswagen and Daimler-Benz merged in 1968 to dominate the domestic market (Lieberman, 1977).

According to the Colonna Report, only a few large enterprises engaged in intra-Community mergers. The most notable were Germany's Agfa and Belgium's Gevaert in their 50-50 merger in 1964 and Holland's Hoergoven's 40 per cent stake in Germany's Hoesch which eventually prefigured their merger into Estel in 1972. Instead of superseding the nation-state, the internationalisation of US capital through the agency of FDI had, in fact, increased the degree of State intervention as each European government, with the possible exception of Germany, pursued neo-mercantilist policies in order to protect their respective State-owned enterprises and their private "national champions". By 1970, the total output of American firms in Europe was two and a half times greater than those of their European rivals in the US market. In 1966 alone, the sales of American firms in Europe had exceeded those of their European rivals in the American market by about $30b (Rowthorn, 1975, p.165). In order to reverse this trade imbalance, the EEC was either compelled to accumulate large trade surpluses with third countries or increase their share of the American market.

As paradoxical as it might appear, the US economy experienced growing current account deficits as soon as American firms began exporting capital. Under the fixed exchange rate regime of the Bretton Woods Agreements, the US could act as "world banker" and issue its own currency which performed the dual functions of an international means of payments and as a principal reserve currency. In other words, the US economy enjoyed the privileges of international financial seigniorage. Seigniorage can be defined as the financial gains accrued to a country that issues an international currency. This can take the form of acquiring foreign assets through a depreciating currency or the gains associated with an inflationary policy which transfers resources from both residents and non-residents who possess US dollars to the US government which issues the money. In its strictest definition, seigniorage refers to the ability of a reserve currency nation to perform the role of world banker. The US economy was therefore capable of exporting capital by accumulating short-term current account deficits since, unlike the rest of the capitalist world, it was relatively unencumbered by the external balance of payments constraint. Similarly, American financial markets could borrow in the short-term in order to lend in the long-term (Parboni, 1981).

Unlike the US, European countries did not enjoy the benefits of seigniorage and could not export capital unless they had accumulated substantial trade surpluses. By the late 1960s, Germany and Italy began to experience growing trade surpluses. Indeed, the combined trade surpluses of the EEC had exceeded the level of American direct investment in Europe as early as 1967. After the wages explosion of the late 1960s, European wage levels began to approach those of the United States. Consequently, the comparative advantage offered by lower European wages no longer applied and the emergence of trade surpluses provided the conditions for the export of capital from Western Europe. In the course of the next decade, European capital pursued an offensive strategy to challenge their American rivals in world markets. Indeed, the American market emerged as the largest export and investment outlet for European TNCs. In stark contrast to the spectre of industrial colonisation evoked in Europe by economic nationalists like de Gaulle and writers like Servan-Schreiber, the American challenge provided a catalyst for the internationalisation of European capital.

The post-war period has doubtless been characterised by the globalisation of the national capitalist economies. The prime agent in this transformation has been the transnational corporation in which the export of capital through the agency of FDI has increasingly eclipsed the export of commodities in order to circumvent trade barriers. Under the aegis of American politico-military hegemony, trade liberalisation was fostered which facilitated the exponential growth of international investment. By 1971, US direct investment abroad was estimated at $86b or five times its 1950 level. In 1966 the value of FDI within the OECD was estimated at $90b of which $54.5b was accounted by US firms. The growth of the Eurodollar and Eurobond market was even more spectacular; in only five years after 1969, the estimated net size of the Eurocurrency market had grown from $44b to $145b. Between 1963 and 1968, the international bond market had increased its volume by over 900 per cent (BIS, 1974). Bukharin's thesis in 1918 appears quite pertinent in the post-World War Two era:

> In various ways there thus takes place the transfusion of capital from one "national" sphere into the other; there grows the intertwining of "national capitals"; there proceeds the "internationalisation of capital"....It grows in volume; it sends part of the surplus value "home" where it may begin an independent movement; it accumulates the other part; it widens over and over again in the sphere of its application; it creates an ever thickening network of international interdependence (Bukharin, 1975, p.26).

The theoretical question posed by whether the internationalisation of capital either increases the interventionist role of the State in order to recover a perceived loss of national sovereignty, or if this process supersedes the nation-state itself, appears to be misguided. The outcome of the relationship between international capital and the nation-state will depend on the specific political and economic configuration, or the existing relations of economic and political power between the two historical agents. The national States themselves either assimilate the interests of international capital into their own national imperatives, or oppose individual foreign corporations in order to protect their domestic firms. The relationship will therefore depend on several scenarios: (1) relations of political and economic power between the international firm and the host country, (2) the inter-state relations between the client State and the State of origin of the international firm and (3) the convergence or divergence of the economic interests between nation-states and international capital. In the latter case, the States themselves will attract foreign investment and preside over the expanded reproduction of capital within their respective national formations (Poulantzas, 1974). Whereas relations between metropolitan or "core" States will necessarily be characterised by relative equality and a degree of reciprocity, those between the "core" and "peripheral" States will be governed by relations of dominance and subordination. The Community constitutes a metropolis or a centre of capitalist accumulation. Its relationship with the US is thus one of relative equality. The creation of a "United States of Europe", however, still remains a distant ideal. In reality, the existing system of European nation-states acted on the behalf of their respective international firms and assimilated the subsidiaries of US corporations in accordance to their own national imperatives. In Marxist terminology, the political "superstructure" of the EEC did not correspond to the existing national economic formations which constituted the "base".

II. The Dollar Crisis

The demise of the international monetary system under the aegis of the Bretton Woods Agreements was a seminal event in the early experiments toward European Monetary Union (EMU). With the collapse of the fixed exchange rate system based on gold/dollar convertibility, international confidence in the dollar evaporated which hastened an international exchange rate crisis. In stark contrast to the dollar shortage of the early post-war years, the US dollar had flooded world markets by the late 1960s.

This enormous expansion of international liquidity was accentuated by the permissive financing of the Vietnam War as the US Treasury resorted to the printing press (Block, 1977). It was the emergence of US balance of payments deficits, however, which ultimately caused a loss of confidence in the US dollar as an international reserve currency and as a means of payments. This flight from the dollar led to a serious drain on US gold reserves which shrank from an estimated \$23b in 1950 to about \$12b in 1967 (Business Week, 1973, p.59). At the same time, official and private foreign dollar holdings increased from \$15.1b in 1957 to \$31.5b in 1968 (Gilpin, 1979, pp. 369-70). The culmination of the gold drain and the loss of confidence in the US dollar induced an unprecedented rise in the demand and market price for gold which eventually destroyed gold/dollar convertibility. Seigniorage of the dollar had been accepted by foreign economic agents as long as it fostered the expansion of international trade. Yet the cohesion and stability of the fixed exchange rate system was ultimately dependent on the ability and willingness of US authorities to act as a world central banker. As soon as their liabilities in the issuing of US dollars were no longer regarded as "good as gold", the "solvency" of the US monetary authorities in their role as world bankers was imperilled (Guerrieri & Padoan, 1986). In short, the success of the system was too highly dependent on the capacity and willingness of the US monetary authorities to perform the role of world banker (Triffin, 1961).

The relative decline of American industrial productivity and international competitiveness contributed to the erosion of its role as reserve currency nation. Close analogies with the demise of the gold standard under the aegis of *Pax Britannica* can be drawn. Just as the decline of Britain's relative economic power had hastened the dissolution of the gold standard, so too the relative decline of US economic power undermined its role as international central banker under the Bretton Woods system. Between 1950 and 1971, US productivity growth had fallen behind the EEC by 35 per cent and Japan by as much as 60 per cent. During the same period, average annual productivity growth in the US was estimated at only 1.7 per cent, compared to 4.5 per cent in the EEC and 10.6 per cent in Japan (Kaldor, 1978, p.64). After the demise of the Bretton Woods system, successive US governments adhered to a policy of "benign neglect" which allowed the dollar to progressively devalue (Parboni, 1981). In other words, successive dollar devaluations contributed to the restoration of US international competitiveness. Dollar devaluations, however, tended to impart inflationary impulses transmitted through the expansion of international liquidity.

Under the fixed exchange rate system, only one country can set its monetary and exchange rate policies independently of all other countries. In the monetary literature this is defined as the *N-th country* paradox. If one assumes that a group of countries are governed by a fixed exchange rate regime, only *country N* is theoretically able to fix its exchange rate in relation to countries *N-1*. The *N-th country* therefore performs an anchor role or reference point in an asymmetrical system to which all of the other countries are compelled to align themselves. Under the former Bretton Woods system, the US economy performed this dominant anchor role (Moon, 1982). In the monetary sphere, this privileged position manifests itself in the financial gains accrued through seigniorage. Despite the demise of the fixed exchange rate regime, the US dollar continued to perform the role of international means of payments and reserve currency. Indeed, the US was no longer constrained by its obligations to accumulate trade surpluses in order to defend gold/dollar convertibility. It was now possible for the US monetary authorities to pursue reflationary policies and dollar devaluations in order to restore their international competitiveness (Parboni, 1981). The relatively small tradeable sector of the US economy as measured as a share of GDP, implied that successive devaluations of the dollar were more inflationary overseas than within the domestic economy. In this sense, the US economy was capable of "exporting" inflation through an increase in international liquidity. Its major industrial rivals were more vulnerable to the inflationary consequences of US expansionary policies.

In Western Europe, these policies had an adverse impact in terms of the inflationary effects and the exchange rate instability generated by speculative financial flows. It was in this volatile environment that General de Gaulle demanded a return to the gold standard. West Germany and Japan, however, were willing to finance the US balance of payments deficits in order to preserve the Western military alliance (Gilpin, 1975, p.154). As the dollar crisis deepened, exchange rate volatility within the Community threatened further progress toward closer economic union. Exchange rate concertation became necessary to prevent a general drift toward competitive devaluations and economic nationalism. The dollar crisis thus spurred European leaders to construct a zone of monetary stability across the Atlantic (Kruse, 1980).

The exponential growth of the private Eurodollar market was the most visible manifestation of this unregulated expansion of international liquidity and credit-creation (Aglietta, 1982). After the demise of the gold/dollar regime, demand for liquidity increased as both international firms and central banks resorted to the Eurodollar market as a source of credit. The origins of this market can be traced back to the Kennedy administration in which the Federal Reserve Bank had imposed limits on interest rates to deposits within the domestic economy (Kindleberger, 1984, p.445). With the restoration of currency convertibility in 1958, financial institutions in Europe could purchase US bonds and securities and engage in foreign exchange transactions. Since investors could earn a higher rate of return by transferring their funds from the US to the Eurodollar market, the growth of the latter was set in motion. The magnitude of this flight of capital was reflected in the expansion of US banks operating abroad; by 1972 there were 107 banks with total assets exceeding $80b. Two years later, this figure had increased to an estimated $140b or equivalent to one fifth of the value of the US national product (Mayer, 1974, p.437). Most of the transactions of the Eurodollar market occurred in the London branches of US banks who would issue "certificates of deposits" against the payment of their dollar liabilities in the US. Since US banks retained possession of dollars deposited abroad, the growth of lending in US dollars by international financial agents generated a multiplier effect and increased the volume of international liquidity. The Eurodollar market therefore acted as a transmission belt in the expansion of international liquidity and contributed to the inflationary upsurge of the 1970s.

Consequently, the entire pyramid of credit was no longer governed by the regime of regulation based on gold/dollar convertibility. A more laissez faire system had emerged based on what Triffin described as the "paper dollar" standard (Triffin, 1987). Despite the demise of the Bretton Woods system, the US balance of payments and domestic US interest rates continued to act as the unofficial pivot by which international liquidity was likely to behave. A rise in US interest rates relative to average international rates was more than likely, *ceteris paribus,* to have a contractionary effect on international liquidity. Conversely, a relative fall in US interest rates would impart an expansionary impetus to international liquidity. This inverse relationship depends quite critically on the continuation of the strategic role performed by the US dollar in international trade and payments. In the absence of the regulatory function performed by a fixed exchange rate regime, both private and public debts have become increasingly monetised. In short, the expansion of international liquidity has mirrored the growth of international indebtedness.

The cessation of gold/dollar convertibility did not necessarily imply the demise of the strategic international role of the dollar. Indeed, the expansion of international liquidity had more than quadrupled in the decade after the collapse of the Bretton Woods system (Triffin, 1978). US trade deficits were no longer financed by the depletion of US reserves but by the acceptance of central banks of US treasury bonds and debts in the form of international reserves. These international reserves had more than doubled between 1970 and 1972 alone (Triffin, 1978, p.53). The US dollar continued to reign supreme as the world's foremost reserve currency, as the principal intervention currency by central banks and as the major numeraire in international transactions. The emergence of this free market system, however, bred speculation, exchange rate volatility and inter-State rivalry over markets and investment outlets. A relatively stable hegemonic regime was replaced by an oligopolistic system driven by competition and rivalry between the US, Japan and the EEC.

Conclusion

The rapid internationalisation of capital had intensified inter-State economic rivalry. With the demise of the post-war Bretton Woods system of fixed exchange rates and dollar/gold convertibility, international financial markets were thrown into turmoil. Speculative capital flows and exchange rate instability threatened to degenerate into competitive devaluations and the re-emergence of economic nationalism. With the onset of trans-Atlantic rivalry, the EEC represented an organised trading bloc in order to enlarge the sphere of accumulation for European corporations (Mandel, 1975). Economic competition from predominantly US corporations demanded a supranational response. European capitalism, however, was still based on national accumulation strategies. The exchange rate crises in Europe between 1968 and 1973 had exposed the limitations of these national strategies. As a result, a more coherent supranational framework was perceived as a necessary development in order to recover the loss of efficacy in national economic policies and provide a commercial space by which European capital could counter the American challenge. In this sense, the dollar crisis had provided a powerful catalyst toward closer European economic and monetary union. In order to avert the possible emergence of competitive devaluations and the destructive consequences of economic nationalism, European economic and monetary union would constitute a new phase in the development of an organised trading bloc.

PART II
EUROPEAN MONETARY UNION

5 EMU: The First Experiment; 1970-78

Introduction

To restate a central theme of this study: the evolution of the single market in Europe was primarily governed by international economic and political forces. The American relationship formed the cornerstone of this historical process of development. Although an internal logic of negative integration was partially evident as the European project progressed from a customs union toward closer economic co-operation, this dynamic was driven by the political necessity to insulate themselves from the adverse impact of US economic policies. With the relative demise of *Pax Americana*, trans-Atlantic co-operation was eclipsed by rivalry and competition. This gulf between the EEC and the United States widened in the wake of the dollar crisis, the onset of the severe recession of 1972-75 and the oil price shocks. It was in this volatile environment of exchange rate instability, an inflationary upsurge and the outbreak of financial speculation that hastened European attempts to establish a zone of monetary stability. Exchange rate instability generated a speculative bubble which not only imperilled the CAP but threatened to undermine the entire process of economic integration. The dollar crisis thus reverberated in European financial markets. According to an early proponent of EMU: "Only by creating a substitute for the dollar can Europe free itself from dependence on it, and only through this means can the US correct its balance of payments" (Mundell, 1973, p.155).

I. The Exchange Rate Crises of 1968-69

Before the onset of the dollar crisis, the EEC had been preoccupied with the completion of the customs union and the CAP. Monetary issues were perceived as less urgent. Although the Treaty of Rome had not explicitly endorsed the objective of monetary union, it did propose closer co-ordination of national economic policies (Articles 103-108)). After the restoration of currency convertibility in 1958, the European parliament had convened preliminary discussions exploring the issue of monetary union. Monnet's Action Committee had adopted the Triffin Plan which involved the creation of a European monetary fund to counter short-term, speculative capital flights (Triffin, 1961). Triffin's proposals had cast doubts over the survival of the Bretton Woods accords as early as 1961. At the time, however, these proposals appeared too ambitious for the Commission which had to contend with Gaullist opposition to federalist ideas. Despite these apparent difficulties, the Commission's Action Programme for the Second Stage of European Union had already stated its intention to focus on fiscal, monetary and exchange rate concertation. A Monetary Committee, represented by two delegates from each Member State was established to consult over the co-ordination of central bank policies which was augmented by the monthly meetings of central bank Governors under the auspices of the BIS. The Commission also established the Medium Term Economic Policy Committee in April 1964 to enact five year plans. Informed by the methods of French indicative planning, the Committee would pursue common Community targets of economic growth and the gradual convergence of macroeconomic policies. Neither the Medium-Term Economic Committee, nor the Monetary Committee, however, could galvanise the necessary political consensus to foster these supranational objectives. National prerogatives continued to govern economic policy (Holland, 1975).

As long as international economic growth and trade expansion could be sustained, the imperatives of EMU were less urgent. The post-war international payments system under the aegis of the Bretton Woods system had furnished a high degree of exchange rate stability. As the American economy expanded, it provided an engine of growth and an expanding export market for the OECD countries. In only eighteen months between 1967 and 1968, however, the international economy was thrown into turmoil by three major exchange rate crises: the liquidation of the pound/sterling regime in November 1967, the dollar crisis of March 1968 and the speculative attack on the French franc and German mark in November 1968. At the very epicentre of this financial meltdown was the demise of the fixed exchange rate system based on gold/dollar convertibility. After all attempts to stabilise gold prices had failed, a two-tiered system emerged in which the official price of gold was preserved at $35 per ounce between central banks but the market price was allowed to fluctuate. This system merely bred further speculation. In the meantime, multilateral negotiations had been convened by the Group of Ten industrial countries to devise a new means of issuing international reserves. An agreement was reached to create Special Drawing Rights (SDRs) issued by the International Monetary Fund and managed jointly by the Group of Ten (Spero, 1977, p.48). These proposals ultimately failed to prevent the collapse of the international monetary system. Indeed, the failure to manage the crisis provided the political rationale for the EEC to devise its own monetary system.

The initial catalyst appeared in France in early 1968. In May a general strike paralysed production for a month and provoked a financial panic as France's current account fell from a surplus of Ffr600m to a deficit of over Ffr3b by the end of the year. Accompanied by the dollar crisis, a general loss of confidence in the franc put pressure on the French authorities to devalue. At the same time, the German authorities experienced an enormous inflow of capital which caused the exchange rate to appreciate quite rapidly. Despite the overwhelming evidence in favour of an exchange rate re-alignment, both the French and German authorities refused to modify their respective parities. De Gaulle, in particular, had rejected a devaluation because this would have been tantamount to a declaration of failure in the government's economic policies. Both governments resorted to fiscal measures and the imposition of capital and exchange rate controls as a means of adjustment. Although these measures temporarily restored confidence, the underlying trade imbalance continued to deteriorate. After the resignation of de Gaulle in April 1969, the new government, led by Pompidou, finally succumbed to a devaluation of 11.1 per cent in August. (Salvati, 1981, p.332). In the meantime, the newly elected Social Democratic government of Herr Brandt in West Germany was obliged to float the mark in October.

II. Proposals for Exchange Rate Concertation

Quite clearly, the exchange rate crisis of 1968-69 had exposed the limitations of existing methods of co-operation between Community central banks. It became evident that when confronted by the sheer size of the private Eurodollar market, national reserves had been dwarfed and governments were eventually forced to make the necessary exchange rate adjustments. The Bundesbank had provided over DM4.5b to the French monetary authorities in 1968 to defend existing parities (Kruse, 1980, p.41).

Despite this financial aid, both governments continued to be at the mercy of speculators. The process of adjustment was too cumbersome and dependent on political decisions which would delay the appropriate response and breed further uncertainty. Short-term credit to deficit countries was neither automatic nor efficient. A more efficient mechanism was therefore required which would prevent delays and establish automatic credit lines. Furthermore, a Community reserve fund would not only bolster reserves to defend exchange rates against speculative attacks, but could also provide the basis for a possible currency bloc to counter the gyrations of the US dollar.

The French government had blamed much of the crisis on US exchange rate and monetary policies. De Gaulle had resented US private agents acquiring French assets with overvalued "paper" dollars. These perceptions were reinforced by the two Barre Plans which sought to elevate the Community's monetary profile on the international stage. In this sense, the first Barre Plan in February 1969 represented the first coherent blueprint for EMU. The Report recommended that progress should be pursued in the co-ordination of macroeconomic policies and the creation of a mutual assistance fund to aid members in the event of an exchange rate crisis. Even though the Barre Report had rejected the creation of supranational institutions and a European central bank, it was still considered too interventionist by the German monetary authorities. The Bundesbank was quite reluctant to compromise its independence. After a series of intense negotiations, a few of the recommendations were adopted by the Council of Finance and Economic Ministers in January 1970. In the final agreement, proposals for closer co-ordination of short and medium term macroeconomic policies were adopted as well as the creation of a short-term credit facility endowed with a fund of two billion dollars which would be deployed against speculative attacks on national currencies.

Despite these concessions, the Barre Plan encountered West German opposition. As the principal creditors, the West German monetary authorities had opposed any further increase in the credit facility to stabilise intra-Community exchange rates. Their greatest concern was the inflationary impact of the inflow of US dollars and were reluctant to use the DM as an international reserve currency. Indeed, the Bundesbank had imposed restrictions on the DM as an international means of payments and had adhered to a strategy of sterilising the inflow of capital. The election of the Social Democratic-Liberal alliance in 1969, however, witnessed a reversal of Germany's former resistance to closer monetary union. Chancellor Brandt was an enthusiastic advocate of EMU as a means to preserve German export markets in Europe and as a defensive mechanism to counter the destabilising impact of dollar devaluations. Convened by the European Heads of State, the Hague Summit in December 1969 provided Chancellor Brandt with the opportunity to promote EMU. The Hague Summit established a Committee, chaired by Pierre Werner of Luxembourg, to devise a strategy for EMU. Released in October 1970, the Werner Report recommended that monetary union should be accomplished over a ten year time frame involving three progressive stages. In its final form, monetary union would exhibit the following attributes:

- A single currency achieved through the elimination of margins of fluctuation and the irrevocable fixing of exchange rates.
- The liberalisation of capital markets within the Community.
- The pooling of national reserves and the creation of a federal system of central banks.
- The centralisation of economic policies under the auspices of supranational institutions attached to the European Parliament and the Commission.

The first stage was scheduled over three years in which exchange rate movements would be narrowed within the agreed margins of fluctuation. This would be followed by the second stage over the next three years in which medium-term economic policies would be harmonised and a European Monetary Co-operation Fund (EMCF) would be established to co-ordinate central bank open market operations and sterilisation policies. The EMCF would gradually increase its supervisory powers over the agreed exchange rate margins of fluctuation. In the final stage, there would be the irrevocable locking of exchange rates and the EMCF would perform the technical functions of a European central bank and eventually issue a single currency. This would be accompanied by closer co-ordination of national fiscal policies and the liberalisation of capital markets. In order to promote a more balanced economic development, there would be a strengthening of structural and regional policies. In its more controversial recommendations, the Werner Report had proposed the creation of supranational institutions which would eventually override national economic policies. Economic and monetary union thus implied political federation.

The implicit federalist elements of the Werner Report proved difficult to reconcile with both the French and German positions, while the issue of the transfer of executive powers would require a radical revision of the Rome Treaties. Differences over the types of strategy to adopt towards EMU had already emerged between the French and German representatives during the Hague Summit. These diverging views were to crystallise into two major camps in subsequent negotiations. The "monetarists" were associated with representatives from France, Belgium and Luxembourg and had advocated a rapid transition towards monetary union. The "economists", on the other hand, were represented by German and Dutch experts who proposed a more gradualist approach which would involve closer economic convergence as a pre-condition to monetary union. In an attempt to reconcile these divergent views, the Werner Committee adopted a strategy of "parallelism" in which economic and monetary union would be pursued simultaneously. The overriding monetary objective, however, was unequivocal as page five of the Report states:

> A unified monetary zone implies the convertibility of currencies, the elimination of margins of fluctuations between parities and the complete freeing of capital movements. This can be achieved by keeping the existing national currencies or by establishing a common currency. Technically the choice would appear unimportant. However, psychological and political considerations would strongly support the adoption of a single currency thus generating the irreversibility of the action.

The economist/monetarist divide was more an expression of conflicting national imperatives than a clash over competing economic theories. The most comprehensive statement of the "monetarist" case was expressed in the second Barre Plan of March 1970 (Appendix A). Unlike the Werner Plan, the pooling of national reserves and the creation of a European monetary fund would be achieved as part of the first stage. Furthermore, central bank interventions would be made in a European "unit of account" instead of the US dollar. The "monetarists" therefore sought to preserve national sovereignty over fiscal policies but project a unified monetary response to the rest of the world. The origins of the "economist" strategy can be identified with the Schiller Plan, submitted to the Council in February 1971. The West German Economics Minister proposed the realisation of economic and monetary union through four progressive stages involving the convergence of national macroeconomic policies with specific targets set for national inflation rates and interest rate differentials. In the final stage, a federal system of central banks would be established which would issue a single currency modelled on the independent Charter of the Bundesbank (Appendix B).

At stake in these debates was the issue of which countries should incur the greatest burden of adjustment. While the Bundesbank was unwilling to surrender its virulent anti-inflationary stance in the event of monetary union, the French authorities were less willing to sacrifice their high levels of economic growth. These divisions doubtless reflected a more general incompatibility between the economic policies of the two countries. The post-war German economic strategy had been inherently anti-Keynesian relying instead on the "social-market" economy to stabilise the business cycle. This was in contrast to the Keynesian policies and economic planning of the French State which fostered an environment of relatively cheap credit to stimulate industrial development and the rapid expansion of domestic demand. The French authorities were thus more willing to tolerate higher inflation in order to achieve higher rates of economic growth and employment, whereas the German authorities adhered to a stringent anti-inflationary policy and a strategy of export-led growth. Between 1950 and 1975, the rate of inflation was estimated at 42 per cent higher in France than in West Germany (Hall, 1984, p.31). Although the French strategy of rapid capital accumulation was quite successful, it also induced recurrent balance of payments problems and successive devaluations. The Germans, on the other hand, experienced growing trade surpluses and the propensity for their exchange rate to appreciate. It was this fundamental incompatibility between the economic strategies of France and Germany that informed the debates over the issue of structural adjustment in the event of monetary union. In order to shed some theoretical insights into these problems, it might be useful to discuss the economic rationale which has informed the theory of Optimum Currency Areas (OCAs).

III. The Theory of Optimum Currency Areas

The seminal theory of OCAs has been attributed to the analysis formulated by R.A. Mundell (1961). The theory is based on a simple two country/region model. It is assumed that countries A and B possess separate national currencies which operate under a fixed exchange rate regime and that both are in a state of balance of payments equilibrium and full employment. If a shift in demand occurs from country B to country A, then B will experience unemployment and A will, *ceteris paribus*, experience an increase in inflation. Insofar as prices are allowed to rise in A, the shift in the terms of trade will enable B to adjust through an exchange rate devaluation and by doing so, avoid incurring the main burden of adjustment in terms of employment and output. However, if country A pursues an anti-inflationary policy, the whole burden of adjustment will be borne by country

B which will tend to experience a higher level of unemployment and a fall in output.

> The policy of surplus countries in restraining prices therefore imparts a recessive tendency to the world economy on fixed exchange rates or (more generally) to a currency area with many separate currencies...In a currency area comprising different countries with national currencies the pace of employment in deficit countries is set by the willingness of surplus countries to inflate. But in a currency area comprising many regions and a single currency, the pace of inflation is set by the willingness of central authorities to allow unemployment in deficit areas (Mundell, 1961, pp.656-57).

Mundell's argument in this regard is quite pertinent to the role performed by Germany under a fixed exchange rate regime in Europe. Since Germany constitutes the principal surplus country, the willingness of the German monetary authorities to reflate and provide an increase in demand for the Community as a whole will play a pivotal role. In the event of a supply shock or a recession, the behaviour of the Bundesbank will be critical in terms of which countries incur the greatest burden of structural adjustment. Under the former Bretton Woods system, the problem of structural adjustment was supervised by the IMF which would intervene in its role as "lender of last resort" to ensure that inflationary deficit countries pursued internal adjustment by adopting an anti-inflationary policy rather than resorting to an external adjustment through an exchange rate devaluation. As a fixed but flexible exchange rate system characterised by a crawling peg, the Bretton Woods system was inherently asymmetrical though this was offset by the willingness of the US monetary authorities to pursue expansionary policies and perform the role of reserve currency nation by providing the necessary liquidity (Tsoukalis, 1985).

It was precisely the problem of structural adjustment which had informed debates between "monetarists" and "economists". In other words, if an OCA is established, which countries or regions would experience the greatest burden of structural adjustment? The "economist" strategy implied that the burden of adjustment would be imposed almost entirely on the deficit countries. Germany would emerge as the de facto nominal exchange rate anchor by virtue of the fact that the DM would tend to appreciate and provide a strong currency option for the system as a whole. The deficit countries, on the other hand, would be compelled to adopt more stringent anti-inflationary policies in order to align themselves to the low German rate of inflation. The convergence of economic policies would therefore tend to conform with the German preferences and impart a deflationary bias within the OCA. The "monetarist" strategy, on the other hand, implied a more symmetrical arrangement with the immediate pooling of reserves which would have shared the burden of adjustment. In this schema, however, there did not exist a mechanism or set of rules that would have prevented the transmission of inflation from the deficit to the surplus countries. In the absence of an IMF-style regulatory framework, the only resolution to the problem of structural adjustment would continue to depend on the willingness of the surplus countries or regions to either reflate or recycle their surpluses in the deficit countries/regions.

An OCA, however, is quite different from complete economic and monetary union. Whereas an OCA consists of a group of countries which share a fixed exchange rate, economic and monetary union implies the convergence and progressive centralisation of macroeconomic policies. It also implies a certain degree of fiscal federalism in order to redistribute resources to the less developed regions. In the absence of these redistributive policies, monetary union would tend to sharpen these regional inequalities. According to Mundell, factor mobility provides the rationalising dynamic in the formation of an OCA. Labour mobility is identified as the ultimate solution to the problem of structural adjustment. If labour migrates from the deficit to the surplus regions, the burden of exchange rate adjustment could be eased, if not eliminated altogether. Mundell also assumes that the liberalisation of capital markets would attract capital away from the high wage regions to the low wage regions.

Mundell's neo-classical assumptions can be criticised on the grounds that the degree of labour mobility in Europe has been relatively rigid across national frontiers. The only notable exception has been the wave of post-war migration of workers from the Italian *mezzogiorno* to the northern industrial core regions in France and Germany. In fact most of the recent migration has originated from the extra-Community regions in northern Africa and Turkey. As long as linguistic impediments continue to exist, labour will continue to remain relatively immobile. Research by Magnifico (1971) suggests that monetary union could be undermined if economic growth and development is not promoted in the less developed regions. In terms of capital mobility, the historical evidence is ambiguous but suggests that capital is more likely to be attracted and concentrated in the more developed "core" regions in which there is a virtuous circle of investment, savings and employment growth (Seers & Vaitsos, 1980).

The problems confronting the issue of monetary union appear to be substantial in the light of diverging national economic policies, uneven development and the structural adjustment required to promote exchange rate concertation between surplus and deficit countries. Although the theory of OCAs highlights some of these issues, the eventual outcome will ultimately depend on the willingness of national governments to surrender a real or perceived sovereignty over monetary and exchange rate policies. The emergence of the dollar crisis and its global repercussions merely brought these issues into sharper focus.

IV. The "Snake in the Tunnel"

Before the official abandonment of the Bretton Woods Agreements in 1972-73, the Community found itself disunited and unable to formulate a common approach to the impact of exchange rate volatility and the speculative flights of capital. While West Germany and Italy had allowed their currencies to float, France adopted a two-tiered regime in which all transactions on the current account were regulated but the capital account was allowed to be determined by the market (Tsoukalis, 1977, p.133). The Benelux countries, in the meantime, had adopted a joint float and had unsuccessfully proposed a joint Community float against the dollar. These discordant and disparate responses to the dollar crisis merely increased the scope for speculation.

The Six were eventually able to reach a tentative accord in their negotiating stance during the Smithsonian Agreements in December 1971. The outcome of these negotiations between the Group of Ten industrial countries involved the official renunciation of gold/dollar convertibility and the unilateral devaluation of the US dollar by nine per cent. As a result, the German mark was effectively revalued by 13.5 per cent, the Belgium franc and Dutch guilder by 11.6 per cent, the French franc by 8.6 per cent and the Italian lira by 7.5 per cent in relation to the US dollar. The Group of Ten also agreed to a modified version of fixed exchange rates which would allow managed, adjustable parities. Parity bands would be increased from the Bretton Woods margin of 1.5 per cent to 2.25 per cent in order to ease speculative propensities.

During the Paris Summit convened by the Heads of Government in February 1972, it was agreed to foster exchange rate concertation between Community Member States by implementing the Smithsonian parities. It soon became evident, however, that the Smithsonian parities set at 2.25 per cent in relation to the dollar implied a margin of intra-EEC currency fluctuation of 4.5 per cent. Furthermore, under a "crawling peg" regime, the spread between two EEC currencies could reach as high as 9 per cent in the long term if one currency appreciated by the permitted 4.5 per cent while another currency depreciated by the same magnitude. Quite clearly, the magnitude of these exchange rate divergences was too high to sustain the CAP and threatened to sabotage further progress toward economic union. The Basle Agreement by the Community central banks in March reduced intra-EEC exchange rate fluctuations to 2.25 per cent which was equivalent to the central dollar margin. It was from this Agreement that the "snake in the tunnel" was born. The parameters of the "tunnel" was set at 4.5 per cent, while the "snake" was confined to a margin of 2.25 per cent. In order to keep the snake within the tunnel, European currencies would be used as a means of central bank intervention while the dollar would be deployed to prevent the snake from leaving the tunnel altogether. The six original members of the currency bloc were soon accompanied by Ireland, the UK, Denmark and Norway.

Despite the Smithsonian accords, further speculative waves engulfed international currency markets in February-March and June-July, 1972. In June a speculative attack was launched against the British pound in the wake of the worsening UK balance of payments. Large scale intervention by the Bank of England in concert with the Banque de France and the monetary authorities in Brussels failed to prevent the British withdrawal from the snake mechanism. The premature exit of the pound after only three months had exposed the institutional weakness and limited resources devoted to defend the snake regime. Encouraged by the capitulation of the European monetary authorities, speculators now targeted the Italian lira and Danish kroner.

In response to the exchange rate crisis, the Finance Ministers of the enlarged Community met in Rome to discuss progress toward the second stage of the Werner Plan. At the top of their agenda were plans to increase the supervisory powers and the financial resources of the European Monetary Co-operation Fund (EMCF). During the speculative attack on the pound, the Bundesbank had refused to support central bank, open market operations because of the British insistence that debts incurred should be repaid in US dollars. In order to sterilise the inflow of US dollars in exchange for DMs, the Bundesbank was willing to allow the pound to float outside the snake mechanism (George, 1991, p.172). The role of the EMCF which had been established in February, was quite negligible in countering these speculative forces. Endowed with a very modest fund of about two billion dollars which was composed of 70 per cent national currencies, 10 per cent gold and 20 per cent US dollars, the EMCF was limited to providing short-term credit to central banks under the auspices of the Bank for International Settlement (BIS). As an agent of the BIS, its autonomy was curtailed and the fund did not have the authority to act as a regional version of the IMF, nor as an embryonic European central bank. Although a degree of consensus had emerged during the Rome meeting to increase funds for the EMCF, the issue of pooling national reserves continued to pose the greatest obstacle to further progress toward monetary union (Coffey, 1977).

In late 1972 European interest rates increased sharply in relation to prevailing rates in the US which attracted another speculative inflow of capital. On this occasion, the Italian lira was the target of a speculative attack. Although the Italian balance of payments was in surplus, the combination of a political crisis and rising German interest rates caused a flight of capital. Despite attempts by the Banca D'Italia to stem the outflow, the lira was forced to abandon the currency peg. At the same time, confidence in the dollar had not been restored as the US current account deficit exceeded $US10b in early 1973. After a series of meetings between the Finance Ministers of the Group of Ten, the US dollar was devalued by 10 per cent in February 1973. The second dollar devaluation signalled the demise of the Smithsonian accords and the international post-war system of fixed exchange rates. The US economy was no longer encumbered by the problem of generating a current account surplus with which to finance its capital account deficit. The US trade and budget deficits could be financed by the issuing of bonds and securities which would be purchased by the rest of the world. In other words, US interest rates would act as the sole means of regulating international liquidity while exchange rates would be governed by market forces. American policy-makers could now pursue an unfettered strategy of restoring their international export competitiveness through successive dollar devaluations (Parboni, 1981, pp.89-90).

The dollar crisis therefore not only imparted an inflationary impulse which had forced European governments to impose quite severe deflationary policies, but successive dollar devaluations also threatened to erode the competitiveness of European exports. The Germans, in particular, were caught in a dilemma. On the one hand, the Bundesbank was reluctant to accumulate excessive US dollars because of the inflationary consequences. On the other hand, the Bundesbank was impelled to support the exchange rate of the US dollar by purchasing US bonds. The US Federal Reserve, in the meantime, attempted to persuade their German counterparts to compensate for US balance of payments deficits through a revaluation of the DM. Given this dilemma, the German authorities sought a joint Community float against the US dollar in order to prevent the internationalisation of the mark. These German proposals had encountered opposition from France and Italy a year earlier, both of whom had favoured more stringent capital controls. With the emergence of generalised currency floats, however, this opposition soon evaporated. A joint Community float against the US dollar would benefit German exports within the EEC and foster a de facto DM zone. Moreover, the creation of an area of monetary stability would prevent the possible onset of competitive devaluations within Europe. In March 1973, the remaining members of the "snake in the tunnel" agreed to a joint float.

V. The Impact of the Oil Price Shocks

The singularly most important event which overshadowed all attempts to foster monetary cohesion occurred with the sudden quadrupling of oil prices by the OPEC cartel in mid-1973. Within the Community, the oil price shocks had intensified existing tensions between high inflation, deficit countries and the low inflation, surplus countries and ultimately hastened the withdrawal of France from the snake regime in January 1974. The following Table illustrates the impact of the oil price shocks on the balance of payments within the EEC.

Table 5.1   **Estimated change in the current account of selected EEC countries in 1974 as a result of the increase in oil prices (including secondary effects)**

Country	$US Billion	Percentage of GNP
West Germany	-5.8	-1.6
France	-5.3	-2.1
Belgium/Luxembourg	-1.2	-2.5
Netherlands	-0.9	-1.5
Denmark	-0.9	-2.8
United Kingdom	-4.7	-2.7
Italy	-4.2	-3.0
Ireland	-0.2	-3.3

Source: Kruse, 1980, p.152.

In stark contrast, the lower dependence on oil imports contributed to a sharp improvement in the US balance of payments. Whereas the EEC had relied on more than 60 per cent of their energy requirements through the importation of oil and Japan as high as 75 per cent, the American dependence was less than 50 per cent (Tanzer, 1974, p.128). The emergence of petro-dollar recycling offered considerable benefits for the US economy. Not only were oil transactions denominated in US dollars but a high proportion of the funds generated by OPEC surpluses were invested in US bonds and equities (Al-Chalabi, 1980, p.97). The expanding OPEC markets offered considerable scope for investment and export outlets of which the US economy was the major beneficiary, most notably in the export of armaments to the Middle East. Since US oil corporations dominated Middle East oil output, the repatriation of oil profits contributed to the improvement of the US balance of payments. Between 1972 and 1974, these oil profits were estimated to have increased from $0.8b to over $10b (Petras & Rhodes, 1980, p.101).

The quadrupling of oil prices coincided with the onset of the most severe international recession since the Second World War. Although it did not cause the recession, the oil price shocks accentuated its severity. A net transfer of about two per cent of income from the OECD countries to the OPEC cartel was estimated to have occurred as a result. The most visible impact of these oil price shocks, however, was experienced in the deterioration of the balance of payments of the most oil dependent countries and the subsequent adjustments required to offset the inflationary cost-push effects. Quite severe deflationary policies were imposed which had an adverse effect on employment. The ability of national governments to accommodate these external supply shocks was highly dependent on the relative economic strength of their economies to withstand these shocks. The oil price shocks therefore acted as a profound catalyst in revealing the conflicting economic policies and diverging trends within the Community.

In West Germany, the impact of the oil price rises was absorbed quite easily because of their accumulated trade and fiscal surpluses. This was in contrast to Italy and France where both higher inflation and fiscal deficits made them more vulnerable. In Italy, for instance, the dependence on oil imports was as high as 70 per cent and the effects of the oil price rises was estimated to have caused a 20 per cent decline in the terms of trade or equivalent to 4.5 per cent of GDP (Llewellyn & Potter, 1982, p.522). Whereas the importance assigned to price stability was paramount in West Germany, this political consensus did not exist in Italy or France. Given these divergent economic trends, further progress toward monetary union was postponed. The Council meeting by the Finance Ministers in June 1974 had failed to reach agreement on the pooling of national reserves, the financing of multilateral aid and other issues related to the second stage of the Werner Plan.

The *coup de grace* to the EMU experiment was delivered by the French government in late 1973. The onset of a balance of payments crisis set in motion a speculative attack on the franc which forced the French authorities to withdraw from the "snake in the tunnel" and allow the currency to float. While the French authorities continued to pursue relatively expansionary policies to stimulate growth and employment, their West German counterparts adhered to a more conservative anti-inflationary strategy. These diverging economic trends could no longer be reconciled as the following Table demonstrates:

Table 5.2   **Comparative Economic Indicators between France and Germany, 1972-74**

	Inflation			Economic Growth		
	1972	1973	1974	1972	1973	1974
France	5.9	7.2	14.0	5.6	6.6	4.7
Germany	5.7	7.2	7.0	3.0	5.5	0.5

Source: OECD Economic Surveys, 1972-74.

Given the reluctance of the French authorities to sacrifice economic growth and the unwillingness of the Bundesbank to tolerate a higher rate of inflation, France's departure from the EMU experiment was inevitable. Despite a temporary re-entry in June 1975, the franc was eventually forced to withdraw once again in March 1976. Consequently, the major "monetarist" member of EMU no longer participated while the two major "economist" countries of Germany and the Netherlands remained inside the tunnel. Consequently, the EMU experiment had become nothing more than an exclusive DM-zone.

Conclusion

Conceived in an environment of extreme exchange rate volatility after the collapse of the Bretton Woods system, the "snake in the tunnel" had provided a degree of exchange rate concertation but lacked both the financial resources and the political cohesion to defend intra-Community exchange rate parities. Diverging economic trends eventually destroyed the process of monetary integration as conflicting national imperatives superseded a common strategy. After the French withdrawal, only five of the original nine members remained in the snake mechanism. The snake found itself both mutilated and deprived of a tunnel. With the onset of the international recession and the oil price shocks, these divergent national trends could no longer be reconciled with the logic of monetary union. This was most evident in the diverging rates of inflation between Member States as Table 5.3 illustrates:

Table 5.3   Annual Inflation Rates in the EEC, 1971-75

	Belgium	France	Germany	Italy	N/lands	Britain
1971	4.3	5.5	5.3	4.8	7.5	9.4
1972	5.4	5.8	5.5	5.7	7.8	7.1
1973	7.0	7.3	6.9	10.4	8.0	8.1
1974	12.6	13.6	6.9	19.4	9.5	16.0
1975	12.7	11.6	5.9	17.1	10.2	24.1
Total	49.5	52.2	34.7	71.3	51.2	82.5

Source: OECD Economic Surveys, 1971-75.

From this evidence alone, the lower inflation countries of West Germany, the Netherlands and Belgium remained within the snake mechanism, while the high inflation countries were forced to adopt an independent float. West Germany became the centre of gravity to which the remaining members coalesced around. The Benelux countries and Denmark gravitated toward West Germany because of their close trading relations and the attractions offered by a stable exchange rate anchor to their small, relatively open economies. A polarisation therefore emerged between the low inflation, surplus countries of West Germany and the Netherlands, on the one hand, and the high inflation, deficit countries of Italy, France and the UK, on the other hand. While the former were more successful in stabilising their short-term exchange rate fluctuations, the latter were trapped in a vicious circle of currency depreciations which merely induced higher import prices and an acceleration of inflation. This widening gulf between the two groups of countries is reflected in Table 5.4.

It might be more accurate to surmise from the historical experience of the EMU experiment that its failure reflected a more profound international rivalry between the US and West Germany over export markets and spheres of investment. From the standpoint of the West German authorities, the EMU experiment represented a possible zone of monetary stability against the destabilising impact of the US dollar. In order to counter the adverse effects of an appreciating exchange rate, German industrial capital accelerated the process of industrial upgrading and technological reconversion. Successive US dollar devaluations, however, threatened German exports in Europe. In this sense, the EMU evolved into a de facto DM-zone to counter the threat posed by US exports and investment to traditional German markets. Despite the rapid appreciation of the mark, German trade surpluses were preserved as Table 5.4 illustrates. More than half of these exports were absorbed by their European trading partners. The Bundesbank, however, refused to act as a financial intermediary for the Community as a whole. Given the close relationship between German finance and industrial capital, an anti-inflationary strategy was viewed as the most effective means by which to counter an appreciating exchange rate in order to preserve their export competitiveness. This was quite evident in the policy of sterilisation against the inflow of short-term capital adopted by the Bundesbank and its refusal to act as a de facto European central bank.

Table 5.4   Current Account Balances and Effective Exchange Rates in Europe, 1973-79

	Current Account Balance (Annual Average $ Millions)	Effective Exchange Rates (Percentage Changes)
France	-1,699	-5.7
Germany	4,375	35.8
Italy	382	-39.2
UK	-2,691	-21.6
Netherlands	629	20.0
Benelux	-710	11.8
OECD Europe	-10,991	N/A

Source: Llewellyn & Potter, 1982, p.35.

Germany consolidated its economic dominance in Europe. The success of monetary union thus hinges critically on the strategic role performed by the Bundesbank. The accumulation of structural trade surpluses and the concomitant refusal of the Bundesbank to reflate will tend to impart a deflationary impulse within the Community. If the theory which informs optimum currency areas is assumed to be correct, then the formation of a fixed exchange rate regime will merely accentuate these asymmetrical relations between the deficit and surplus countries in the absence of a German policy of reflation. In this sense, it is the dollar-DM relationship which ultimately constrains Germany's ability to pursue a more expansionary monetary policy regardless of the Bundesbank's historical aversion to inflation. The weakness of the US dollar in relation to the DM will tend to sharpen these intra-Community asymmetries. Conversely, a strong dollar will promote a more symmetrical configuration within Europe, all other things being equal. In the final analysis, however, monetary union has essentially been governed by political imperatives; its ultimate fate rests on the willingness of nation-states to surrender their perceived monetary sovereignty to a supranational organisation.

Appendix A

The Second Barre Plan (March, 1970)

Stage One: 1970-71

- The provision of medium-term aid (using SDRs) and the adoption of a medium-term plan to co-ordinate economic policies.
- The harmonisation of credit policies under the supervision of central bank governors.
- The harmonisation of the VAT and the rules governing capital movements.

Stage Two: 1972-75

- Economic objectives will be determined on the Community level but the creation of a European central bank is rejected.
- The margins of exchange rate fluctuations should be reduced to one per cent either side of parity.

Stage Three: 1976-80

- The Council of Central Bank Governors to determine monetary policies.
- A European reserve fund established.
- The liberalisation of capital markets within the Community.
- The creation of a European unit of account as a means of settlement between central banks.

Appendix B

The Schiller Plan (February, 1971)

Stage One

- The co-ordination of macroeconomic policies in the short and medium terms.
- Short-term monetary targets established and the criteria for the convergence of national interest rates finalised.
- The creation of a short-term credit facility.

Stage Two

- The promotion of a more balanced rate of economic growth through the convergence of national macroeconomic policies.
- A medium-term credit facility established to promote closer exchange rate alignments.

Stage Three

- Community economic policies introduced to override national economic policy instruments.
- A federal reserve system of central banks established.
- An increase in medium-term financial aid to encourage structural adjustment in the less developed regions.
- The partial pooling of national reserves.

Stage Four

The final stage would involve the transfer of monetary and exchange rate policy to a European central bank or a federal system of central banks. Exchange rates would be irrevocably fixed in order to establish the conditions for the issuing of a single European currency.

6 The European Monetary System; 1979-87

Introduction

With the demise of the first experiment in monetary union, many critics had proclaimed that the whole enterprise was ill-conceived and doomed to failure. Another attempt to revive the project was considered highly unlikely as long as the Bundesbank remained trenchantly opposed and asymmetries continued to prevent the convergence of macroeconomic policies. Rumours of its demise, however, were greatly exaggerated. The renewed dollar crisis of 1978 provided a catalyst to launch a second experiment in March 1979. The American policy of "benign neglect" had allowed the dollar to slide which, in turn, generated a renewed phase of international volatility in financial and currency markets. In the course of 1977, the German mark had appreciated by about ten per cent in relation to the US dollar. At the same time, however, the French franc had depreciated by 6 per cent and the Italian lira by a dramatic 15 per cent against the German mark. The obvious threat posed by these re-alignments convinced the newly elected Social Democratic government of Chancellor Schmidt that a new exchange rate regime was required within the Community. This became even more evident after the failure of German-US measures to stabilise the dollar. With the recent election of President d'Estaing of France, Schmidt had found an accommodating ally in reviving the EMU project.

I. The Political Rationale

The earliest proposals for the re-launching of the EMU project came from Roy Jenkins - a former President of the Commission - in October 1977 (Jenkins, 1978). These proposals formed the basis of the Schmidt initiative and the accord reached with D'Estaing in April 1978 at the European Council meeting in Copenhagen. Three months later, at the European

Council meeting in Bremen, the Franco-German proposals were endorsed and the Ministers of Finance were instructed to formulate the institutional and technical details. The legal and institutional structure of the European Monetary System (EMS) were finally adopted by the European Council in Brussels on December 5 and 6, 1978. According to this agreement, the EMS was expected to enter into its formal operational phase within two years of its official launch in March 1979. The Greek and British representatives chose to postpone their membership of the EMS.

In short, the EMS was, like its predecessor, essentially a Franco-German initiative. A similar logic governed the new accord: while the French sought German support for their exchange rate which had come under renewed speculative attack, Germany demanded support for closer co-ordination of national economic policies. In other words, the trade-off involved the French aims of stabilising the CAP and the German desire to prevent the onset of competitive devaluations which would ultimately threaten their industrial exports. However, Schmidt's EMU proposals were trenchantly opposed by the Bundesbank which feared that their independence would be imperilled and inflationary pressures would be rekindled. In order to placate the Bundesbank, Schmidt's plan involved an anti-inflationary bias and strict limits imposed on the use of US dollars in exchange rate interventions. In its rudimentary form, the Schmidt plan had envisaged the following features:

- Exchange rate interventions to be made in Community currencies with stringent limits imposed on the use of dollars.
- Monthly settlement of payments with the debtor incurring the exchange rate risk.
- The introduction of a very short-term credit facility to provide automatic financial aid to Member States experiencing an exchange rate crisis. The fund would be limited to a system of national quotas and all settlements would be made within three months through a European unit of account.
- In order to impose a greater degree of rigour to the process of exchange rate concertation, inflation targets would be set.

The Italian monetary authorities were initially ambivalent about the revival of monetary union. They had been pursuing a strategy which had borne considerable success in promoting the expansion of their exports. This strategy had involved an appreciation of the lira against the US dollar, on the one hand, and a depreciation of the lira against the mark, on the other hand. Consequently, Italian exports had gradually shifted away from the US market and had increased their share of the European market at the expense of France and Germany. Italy's decision to join the EMS was thus primarily motivated by political considerations but conditional on a wider margin of fluctuation of 6 per cent for the lira in the Exchange Rate Mechanism (ERM). From the standpoint of the British authorities, the Franco-German agreement had aroused deep suspicions. They had, doubtless, not easily forgotten their disastrous experience in the "snake" experiment which had witnessed an unprecedented attack on the pound sterling and caused an estimated 30 per cent loss of their foreign reserves. Moreover, with the opening of upstream operations in their North Sea oil venture, the pound had become an oil currency and had appreciated against the EMS currencies. Given these circumstances, the UK authorities postponed their participation in the EMS, although the pound sterling would constitute one of the currencies in the ECU basket. Although the political rationale in re-launching the EMU project was paramount, the underlying economic conditions were also favourable. Between 1978 and 1982 there appeared overwhelming evidence of a convergence of critical economic indicators after the tensions generated by the oil price shocks. This evidence is highlighted in Table 6.1.

Table 6.1   Economic Indicators (1978-82)

	1978	1979	1980	1981	1982
Countries With Low Inflation					
Belgium/Luxembourg [(a)]	-1.0	-2.8	-4.2	-4.1	-3.1
(b)	4.5	4.5	6.6	7.6	8.7
(c)	107.7	104.9	100.8	97.8	88.0
The Netherlands [(a)]	-1.1	-1.3	-1.8	2.0	2.7
(b)	4.1	4.2	6.5	6.7	5.9
(c)	123.5	120.5	117.9	115.9	120.1
West Germany [(a)]	1.4	-0.8	-1.9	-0.9	0.5
(b)	2.7	4.1	5.5	5.9	5.3
(c)	109.3	107.8	102.0	98.4	100.4
Countries With High Inflation					
France [(a)]	1.5	0.9	-0.6	-0.8	-2.9
(b)	9.3	10.6	13.5	13.3	12.0
(c)	94.0	96.1	99.3	101.1	97.0
Italy [(a)]	2.4	1.7	-2.5	-2.3	-1.6
(b)	12.2	14.7	23.0	17.7	16.6
(c)	76.1	78.7	85.9	89.6	92.3

(a) Current Account Balances (Percentage of GDP)
(b) Inflation Rates (Average annual percentage increase)
(c) Real Exchange Rates (1970=100)

Source: OECD Main Economic Indicators, 1983.

II. The Intervention and Financing Mechanisms

Although it is possible to identify a certain degree of continuity between the EMS and its "snake" predecessor, important differences were evident in relation to the role performed by the European Currency Unit (ECU) and the mechanism of the "divergence indicator." Furthermore, the EMS was endowed with more than twice the financial resources to defend agreed parities and was governed by a greater degree of exchange rate flexibility. These institutional features were accompanied by a strengthening of the regional and structural funds; more than 200 billion Ecus were allocated to these funds in the first five years (Coffey, 1987; p.23). The kernel of the EMS was the Exchange Rate Mechanism (ERM) in which participating countries were obliged to keep their bilateral exchange rates within the agreed margins of fluctuation. Although these central rates were expressed in terms of the ECU, the compulsory intervention rates were defined on a bilateral basis. The Brussels resolution states that "in principle, interventions will be made in participating currencies" (Article 3.3) and that "intervention in participating currencies is compulsory when the intervention points defined by the fluctuation margins are reached" (Article 3.4). A central system of bilateral parities was thus established in which intra-ERM margins of fluctuation were limited to within 2.25 per cent either side of parity, with the exception of Italy and Ireland in which the margin was set at (+/-) 6 per cent. Beyond these bilateral limits, compulsory intervention was enforced by the Brussels resolution.

The EMS Agreement was the outcome of a series of political compromises between potential debtors and creditors. The latter were guaranteed lines of credit to defend the agreed parities in order to promote a smooth exchange rate adjustment. The overriding objective of potential creditors, on the other hand, was focused on the domestic monetary consequences of the intervention and financing operations. Their concern was to avoid excessive liquidity and credit creation by imposing specific commitments on the debtor countries to introduce the necessary economic policy adjustments. These provisions were enshrined in the strict limits in the period of repayment under the Very Short-Term Financing facility (VSTF) and by the IMF-type conditionality rules for medium term credit. The use of Ecus was initially confined to 50 per cent of settlements, while members of the VSTF were obliged to deposit 20 per cent of their gold and dollar reserves against the issuing of Ecus. Consequently, both the limited use of Ecus in official transactions and their non-convertibility, had failed to prevent the Community's continued dependence on the US dollar. Indeed, over two thirds of all official interventions between 1979 and 1985 were denominated in the US dollar. Since the ECU was devoid of legal tender status, it was confined merely as a unit of account replacing the former European Unit of Account (EUA).

The EMS was therefore characterised by two major innovations: the Exchange Rate Mechanism (ERM) and the European Currency Unit (ECU). The ERM can be described as an "adjustable peg" regime by which marginal interventions were compulsory. Intra-marginal interventions were also possible and became the most frequent type of market intervention by central banks. These often involved swap agreements between central banks before the compulsory margins were reached. For instance, if the Italian lira depreciated to the lower limits of its permitted band in relation to the German mark, the Bank of Italy was obliged to intervene by selling marks and purchasing lira. Should the lira overshoot the divergence threshold, marginal intervention was compulsory and the VSTF was deployed to provide lines of credit between the central banks in order to avoid destabilising speculation against the lira. Originally it was agreed that the debt should be settled within 45 days after the end of each month but with the signing of the Basle-Nyborg Agreement of 1987, the period of settlement was extended to 75 days.

The other major feature of the EMS was the creation of ECUs which was based on a basket of currencies calculated as a proportion of each member's GDP, trade and short-term credit quotas. Each currency had a central rate expressed in ECUs. These central rates could be changed by a voluntary agreement between the central banks and the EC Commission. By linking together the ECU related central rates, a parity grid could be devised by a series of bilateral rates. In other words, each currency was calculated as a central rate of the ECU rather than in terms of the ECU. As a result, depreciating currencies experienced a fall in their relative weight in the ECU basket while appreciating currencies exhibited an increase. In retrospect, there developed an inherent tendency for strong currencies to gradually increase their relative value in terms of the ECU which eventually entrenched the asymmetrical dynamics of the system.[1]

The most innovative feature of the ECU was the introduction of a "divergence indicator" which measured the extent to which a given currency was approaching its maximum divergence threshold. The indicator was expressed as a percentage. If it reached 75 per cent, the currency had approached its divergence threshold and the monetary authorities were obliged but not compelled to intervene (Appendix A). Since the weight of a particular currency influenced the market rate of the ECU expressed in that currency, the market rate could only deviate from its central rate by a percentage necessarily less than the maximum 2.25 per cent or 6 per cent. As a result, the maximum divergence was higher the smaller the weight of the currency and, conversely, lower the greater the weight of the currency in the ECU basket. Table 6.2 demonstrates these differing maximum spreads and divergence thresholds.

---

[1]   In the Maastricht Treaty of 1992 it was agreed to freeze these bilateral rates.

Table 6.2   Maximum Divergence Spreads and Divergence Thresholds
(Average rates from September 1984 to February 1985)

(1) Currency	(2) Maximum Spread (%)	Divergence Threshold (%) (75% of (2), (+/-))
BRF/LFR	2.06	1.545
DM	1.53	1.148
HFL	2.02	1.515
DKR	2.19	1.643
FF	1.82	1.365
LIT	5.40	4.050
IRL	2.22	1.665

Source: Commission Departments.

In order to issue ECUs, central banks deposited twenty per cent of their gold and dollar reserves with the EMCF. These official ECUs were intended to serve as a reserve asset, though subject to various restrictions. As a non-convertible instrument of credit, ECUs could be used as the official numeraire in intra-ERM settlements. It was envisaged by the EMS agreements that the ECU would promote a more equitable sharing of the risks between creditors and debtors. However, given the "strong currency" option adopted by the weaker members, the EMS evolved into an asymmetrical regime dominated by the deutschmark. Indeed, the growth of private ECUs, not anticipated by the EMS Agreement, has stemmed largely as a substitute for the DM because of the reluctance of the Bundesbank to internationalise the German currency. In an international environment characterised by exchange rate volatility and rising nominal interest rates, the low risk premium of the ECU basket and its lower interest rates for borrowers, increased the demand for private ECUs throughout the 1980s.[2]

---

2   This issue will be discussed in greater detail in Chapter 7.

III. The International Dimension

Although the EMS provided a considerable degree of exchange rate cohesion, it failed to promote monetary sovereignty in relation to the US dollar. Just like its snake predecessor, the survival of the EMS was critically dependent on the DM-dollar relationship. The EMS was thus still vulnerable to exogenous shocks emanating from the volatility of the US dollar. From this standpoint, the relative success of the EMS during the first half of the 1980s was determined, to a large extent, on the sharp appreciation of the US dollar during this period. The objective conditions were favourable in terms of the cyclical recovery in 1982-87 which was accompanied by a fall in oil prices. Intra-ERM exchange rate cohesion and the convergence of economic policies could be fostered in this favourable international environment.

In stark contrast, the US dollar had been subjected to chronic instability in the course of 1977. The prospect of a prolonged deficit in the US current account and the inability of the government to dampen inflationary forces had hastened a renewed dollar crisis. On the other hand, the sharp appreciation of the mark generated tensions within the Community. In response to the slide in the US dollar, the Carter administration was persuaded to abandon their policy of "benign neglect" and actively pursued a more interventionist strategy. With the onset of recession in the late 1970s, the Americans propounded the "locomotive theory" in which they attempted to persuade the major surplus countries of Japan and Germany to pump prime their economies, arguing that a concerted fiscal stimulus would redress the widening trade imbalances and generate a sustained recovery. Both the German and Japanese authorities, however, were quite reluctant to pursue a more expansionary programme because of the inflationary risks involved. In 1977 and 1978, the US economy experienced a current account deficit of $15.2b and $13.2b respectively. At the same time, official claims on the US Treasury increased by around $35b and $32b respectively. In other words, the US Treasury was forced to replenish its reserves by borrowings in foreign capital markets (Thygessen, 1981, p.502). Table 6.3 illustrates these growing trade imbalances between the three major capitalist economies.

Table 6.3   Balance of Trade and the Current Account for
            the US, Germany and Japan, 1977-80 ($US billions)

	1977	1978	1979	1980
USA (1)	-30.9	-33.8	-29.5	-25.0
(2)	-15.2	-13.5	-0.3	0.1
Germany (1)	19.3	15.5	17.7	10.0
(2)	4.3	8.9	-5.8	-15.5
Japan (1)	17.3	24.6	1.8	0.0
(2)	10.9	16.5	-8.6	-10.8

(1) Balance of Trade
(2) Current Account for the US, Germany and Japan

Source: OECD Main Economic Indicators, 1982.

The failure of German-US negotiations to manage the dollar slide posed a serious dilemma for the German monetary authorities. They could either curtail the demand for DM-denominated assets by purchasing US bonds and securities thereby financing the US current account deficit, or they could re-launch the EMU project as a means by which the reserve currency status of the DM would be confined within the Community. The former option would have required excessive intervention by the Bundesbank in close concert with their American counterparts. Given the fact that unsterilised, open market operations were anathema to the Bundesbank because of the excessive creation of liquidity and the inflationary risks involved, agreement over a target zone for the dollar/DM exchange rate was untenable from the standpoint of the German monetary authorities. The second option offered greater strategic advantages. EMU would absorb and deflect demand for DM-denominated assets by making other European currencies closer substitutes for the DM.

Carter's neo-Keynesianism was soon replaced by a more orthodox monetarist strategy with the Presidential victory of Reagan in 1980 and the ascendancy of Paul Volcker as the incumbent Governor of the Federal Reserve Board. With the onset of the second oil price shocks in 1979, the OECD countries were compelled to enact restrictive fiscal and monetary policies which had the effect of dampening the level of effective demand and contributed to the international recession of 1979-82. Germany was especially affected by the oil price rises as the trade balance went into the red in 1979-81. Given these unusual circumstances, the first two years of the EMS were characterised by the relative weakness of the German mark. At the same time, a strong dollar policy was adopted by the Reagan administration. The dollar rose sharply between July 1980 and February 1981, estimated at about 20 per cent on a trade weighted average. US nominal interest rates also rose sharply, attracting a considerable inflow of capital.

Quite contrary to expectations, the German mark did not perform the strong currency option in the first two years of the EMS transitional period. The relative weakness of the mark, however, militated against the inherent asymmetrical tendencies of the system and contributed to the stability and cohesion of intra-ERM exchange rates. These empirical observations lend credence to the contention that the dollar/DM relationship has been absolutely pivotal in the behaviour of the ERM. In other words, if the German mark appreciates against the dollar it will tend to appreciate against the other ERM currencies. Conversely, a relative, nominal depreciation of the mark against the US dollar has imparted a more symmetrical configuration within the ERM. The most plausible explanation for this inverse relationship is the fact that the mark is viewed by international investors and other financial agents as a close substitute for the US dollar. An exchange rate depreciation of the dollar will therefore induce a flight of capital into either mark or yen denominated assets (Padoa-Schioppa, 1984, p.130).

As the EMS jointly floated downwards against the dollar between 1980 and 1985, the American domestic market provided an expanding outlet for European exports which, in turn, imparted a powerful stimulus for the cyclical recovery after 1982. German trade surpluses re-appeared. As the recovery gained momentum, however, the disparities between the surplus poles of Germany and the Netherlands, on the one hand, and the deficit poles of Italy and France, on the other hand, generated an undercurrent of potential conflict. These underlying tensions were temporarily contained by the fall in oil prices and the rapid expansion of the US economy which provided an engine of growth for the OECD countries as a whole. In retrospect, the contradictory US strategy of tight monetary policies accompanied by expansionary fiscal policies which were partly driven by increased military expenditure, could not be sustained as long as the US continued to accumulate a trade deficit. The relative strength of the dollar was not induced by a substantial improvement in the American trade deficit, nor by a recovery of its industrial export competitiveness. Instead, the massive inflow of capital was governed almost entirely by the inducement of high nominal interest rates. Figure 6.1 illustrates short-term interest rate trends between 1975 and 1985 in the United States.

By increasing nominal interest rates and attracting short-term capital, the American economy was absorbing world savings which had a negative impact on world investment, most notably in Europe. This was offset, in the short-term, by an increase in European exports to the American market through a real exchange rate depreciation. In short, a "virtuous circle" had been set in motion in which the US economy provided an outlet for European and East Asian exports, while the savings of the latter were converted into an increase in investment in the United States. This "virtuous circle", however, was only possible as long as the dollar continued to appreciate and protectionist impulses were contained in the United States.

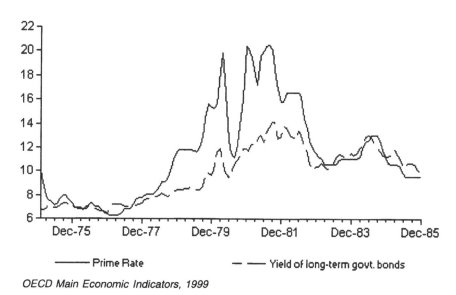

OECD Main Economic Indicators, 1999

Figure 6.1   United States: Interest Rates; 1975-85 (percentage per annum)

The strong dollar policy in the first term of the Reagan administration generated two contradictory outcomes. Although the strong dollar and high nominal interest rates contributed to a curtailment of domestic inflation, it also imparted a negative impact on US export competitiveness which was reflected in the deterioration of the balance of payments. The US trade deficit had increased from an average of $US27b in 1978-80 to $US148b in 1985, while the current account deficit deteriorated from $US4b to about $US128b over the same period (Parboni, 1986). By March 1985, the dollar was estimated to have appreciated by more than thirty per cent on a trade weighted average since the beginning of 1981. International pressure began to mount for a sustained dollar devaluation, especially after the realisation that the US economy had become a net debtor for the first time since the turn of the century. This was accompanied by a growing protectionist sentiment in the US Congress. The Reagan administration could either succumb to these protectionist demands or divert them through a dollar devaluation. In the light of these events, a more interventionist policy emerged in contrast to the prevailing neo-liberal paradigm that had informed US exchange rate policies.

During the second term, the Reagan administration pursued a strategy not too dissimilar to that of the Carter years by attempting to persuade Germany and Japan to adopt more expansionary policies. Predictably enough, the German and Japanese governments were reluctant to accommodate these demands. With the breakdown of macroeconomic policy co-ordination between the major industrial countries (the G-7), the central bankers of these countries launched a series of concerted interventions in order to avert a crash landing of the US dollar. An estimated $US12b was mobilised in March 1985 to engineer a soft landing. Within a year, the dollar had depreciated by 35 per cent on a trade weighted average; the dollar/mark rate had fallen from 3.47 to 2.25 and its yen value from 260 to 175. Figure 6.2 compares the real effective exchange rates of Germany and the United States between 1973 and 1997.

After the Plaza Accords of September 1985, another concerted central bank intervention was orchestrated to counter the mounting speculation in global currency markets. The failure of Germany and Japan to stimulate their economies as the US has requested during the Plaza Summit only provoked US officials to "talk down" the dollar in what soon developed into a dangerous game of monetary brinkmanship (Funabashi, 1988). Although this American strategy eventually persuaded the Japanese to pursue a more expansionary policy after the stock market crash of October 1987, the German authorities remained intransigent. Quite simply, German exports were not as dependent on the US domestic market as those of Japan. Whereas only about ten per cent of German exports were destined for the

American market, the EEC had accounted for about a third of total German exports.

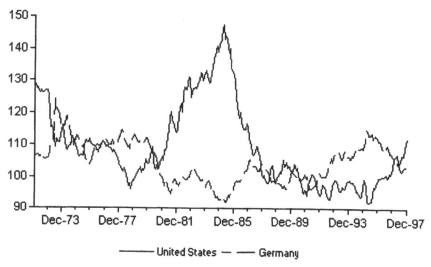

OECD Main Economic Indicators, 1999

**Figure 6.2   Real Effective Exchange Rates: United States
and Germany; 1973-97 (1990=100)**

Consequently, the maintenance of a stable exchange rate regime in Europe, embodied by the EMS, represented the primary German concern and had informed their negotiating stance during the Plaza and Louvre summit meetings. As the dollar rapidly fell from 1985 onwards, a "vicious circle" developed with the onset of inter-State rivalries over markets and investment outlets (Parboni, 1986). It was in this volatile environment that international summits were convened to engineer a "soft landing" of the US dollar and to co-ordinate macroeconomic policies. The ultimate failure of these summits to resolve the basic core of the problem - US deficits and dollar instability - hastened widespread financial panic in world financial markets which culminated in the stock market crashes of 1987 and 1989.

The sharp decline of the US dollar had intensified tensions within the EMS. Although the first major re-alignment in April 1986 was managed quite smoothly, the second major re-alignment in January 1987 caused a minor eruption as the French franc fell below the divergence threshold. The EMS central banks mobilised over $US10b in open market operations to preserve parities. The weakness of the dollar therefore rebounded within the EMS. Yet despite these external shocks, the EMS experiment had survived. Its internal cohesion had withstood one of the most turbulent episodes in post-war financial history. The extent to which this cohesion and stability could be preserved, however, hinged on the strategic role performed by Germany.

Conclusion

Conceived as a Franco-German accord between President d'Estaing and Chancellor Schmidt, the EMS signalled a high point in the construction of the European edifice and became the blueprint for the modern evolution of the Euro. Despite initial resistance from the Bundesbank, the internal financial mechanisms of the EMS provided a more coherent and flexible means of exchange rate concertation than its "snake' predecessor. Despite these innovations, the first decade of the EMS experiment suggests that its relative success was largely due to a favourable international environment. Most of the period (1978-85) was characterised by a strong dollar, falling oil prices and a sustained international recovery from the recession of 1979-82. The US economy acted as the engine of growth for the European recovery as a virtuous circle was set in motion by which European exports increased their penetration of the American market, while the US attracted a net inflow of investment from Europe and Japan. The reversal of these propitious, external factors with the onset of the severe recession of the early 1990s signalled the demise of the EMS experiment. Quite apart from the first two years of the EMS, the German mark re-emerged as the nominal exchange rate anchor for the system as a whole. The economic and political implications of Germany's pre-eminent role will be explored in the next chapter.

Appendix A

The Divergence Indicator

The "divergence indicator" is calculated in two stages:

(1) By calculating the premium (P) or discount (D) shown by the market rate of the ECU in terms of that currency against its ECU-related central rate.

(2) By comparing the result obtained with the maximum divergence spread (MDS). The MDS for each currency is assigned an index of 100. A currency therefore reaches its divergence threshold when the index is 75.

Expressed as a formula, the indicator is calculated as follows:

$$P \text{ or } D = \frac{\text{ECU market rate - ECU central rate}}{\text{ECU central rate}} \times 100$$

The following example illustrates this equation:
The rate of the Belgium franc on June 17 1982 = 45.2961 (ECU)
The ECU-related central rate of the Belgium franc = 44.9704
The maximum divergence spread of the Belgium franc = 2.9704

Therefore:

$$P = \frac{45.2961 - 44.9704}{44.9704} \times 100 = 72\%$$

$$DI = \frac{0.72}{2.0668} \times 100 = 35$$

7 The Internal Contradictions of the EMS

Introduction

In the study of international political economy, the concept of "hegemony" has acquired a strategic meaning. Whether implicitly or explicitly, the term applies to one country or a group of nation-states which form a dominant power bloc within a definite hierarchy of nation-states. In the "world system" literature this configuration is viewed as a zero-sum game between the dominant core, satellite and peripheral states (Wallerstein, Arrighi, et al). With the end of the Cold War, a tri-polar system of Japan, the European Community and the United States has emerged as the dominant, core group of states. The demise of the post-war system of *Pax Americana* could witness the emergence of trading blocs and exclusive currency zones gravitating around these hegemonic core regions.

> Undoubtedly the fact of hegemony presupposes that account be taken of the interests and the tendencies of the groups over which hegemony is to be exercised and that a certain compromise equilibrium should be formed - in other words, that the leading group should make sacrifices of an economic-corporate kind. But there is no doubt that such sacrifices and such a compromise cannot touch the essential; for though hegemony is ethical-political, it must be economic, must necessarily be based on the decisive function exercised by the leading group in the decisive nucleus of economic activity (Gramsci, 1971, p.161).

Within the European Community, Germany's hegemonic role has been confined to the economic sphere. Since the Second World War, the EC has been successful in mediating between the revival of German economic power and the containment of German politico-military ambitions. The other crucial historical condition was the construction of a European *cordon sanitaire* to counter the perceived threat of Soviet westward expansion. In the post-Cold War era, the survival of these supranational forms of mediation will critically depend on the strategic imperatives of the German State. The realisation of monetary union is therefore closely entwined with these strategic and political issues. A single currency would presuppose the emergence of a de facto DM-zone. In other words, EMU is likely to assimilate and reproduce the German model based on the creation of an independent central bank which emulates the policies and structure of the Bundesbank.

I. Germany and the Problem of Asymmetry

In contrast to the Bretton Woods regime in which the American financial system performed the role of world "central banker" with the issuing of international reserves, the German financial system has remained introverted and firmly anchored with the imperatives of German industrial accumulation. Whereas the US ran successive current account deficits and presided over the export of capital, Germany has accumulated substantial trade surpluses. Even though the export of capital from Germany has increased rapidly over the past two decades, the Bundesbank has been very reluctant to allow the mark to acquire an international reserve currency status. Both the critical mass of the German economy and its close trading relations with other EMS countries places the German economy in a unique position to impose its economic preferences on the final blueprint for monetary union. In this sense, the EMS can be portrayed as a hierarchical regime with Germany at the very apex. The problem of asymmetry is thus closely related to Germany's strategic trade relations within the EMS.

> To mix a metaphor: Germany is at the heart of the European economy, while all the other economies are peripheral. Economically, Europe may be defined as a German zone. This zone includes all countries that send a significant share of their exports (15% or more) to Germany and at least half of their total exports to the German economic zone, including Germany itself. Germany in turn sends half of its exports to the periphery of its economic zone, but no individual country absorbs more than 5-6 per cent of its exports (except Holland and France, each of which account for almost 10 per cent of German exports). This configuration of trade makes economic relations asymmetrical (Parboni, 1981, p.91).

Although the problem of asymmetrical exchange rate relations was acknowledged during the Bremen and Brussels summits which had launched the EMS, the gravitational pull of the German economy has been irreversible. Rather than sharing the burden of adjustment, the main burden has been imposed on the weaker, deficit countries. The Bundesbank has preserved its staunch independence, while Germany has been able to pursue relatively autonomous monetary policies within the EMS but has been constrained by its relationship with the US dollar and US monetary policies. In short, the dollar/DM relationship has ultimately dictated intra-ERM exchange rate alignments. The continued volatility of the dollar and the inflationary consequences of US domestic policies has impelled the ERM countries to peg their currencies to the German mark. As a result, German interest rates have acted as the unofficial anchor or benchmark within the EMS as Figure 7.1 demonstrates.

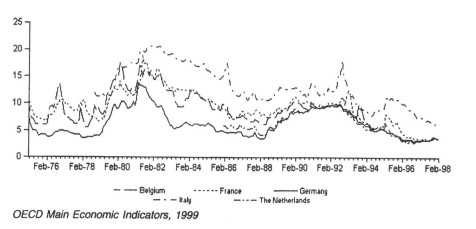

OECD Main Economic Indicators, 1999

Figure 7.1   Short-Term Interest Rates in the EMS; 1975-98
   (3 months, percentage per annum)

While the German monetary authorities were able to determine their exchange rate policies through interest rate adjustments, the deficit countries of France and Italy increasingly resorted to the imposition of exchange rate and capital controls. Insofar as the EMS was characterised by a "crawling peg" regime similar to the Bretton Woods system, central banks were not compelled to enforce parities in the medium and long-term. To be sure, compulsory interventions on the margins through the automatic operation of the VSTF were not very frequent. This appears to suggest that intra-marginal interventions have predominated which implies that the burden of exchange rate adjustment was borne largely by the weaker, deficit members of the EMS.

These empirical observations of the internal dynamics of the EMS support the proposition that there is an inherent asymmetry with Germany acting as the de facto *Nth* country and providing an exchange rate anchor for the system as a whole. The problem of asymmetry, however, is not in itself a major obstacle to the maintenance of exchange rate stability. The real problem lies with the role performed by the *Nth* country. Under the fixed but adjustable exchange rate system of Bretton Woods, the *Nth* country - the United States - provided an expansionary impetus for the system as a whole, while the US financial system was willing and structurally capable of financing the export of capital. By incurring successive current account deficits, the American financial system was acting as a financial intermediary by borrowing in the short-term in order to lend in the long-term. In stark contrast, the German economy has imparted a deflationary tendency within the EMS and its financial sector has been unwilling to act as a financial intermediary for the system as a whole. These constraints have been the product of the DM/dollar relationship and the German structural propensity to accumulate trade surpluses.

In regard to the first constraint, a strong dollar will tend to foster a higher degree of symmetry within the ERM while a weak dollar will impart a greater degree of intra-ERM exchange rate divergence. This inverse relationship is based on the close substitute between the dollar and the mark by international financial agents. The inherently "anti-Keynesian" stance of the Bundesbank has enshrined the objective of price stability as the cornerstone of German macroeconomic policy. By doing so, however, a disinflationary impulse has been transmitted throughout the EMS zone. While the German authorities pursued a trade off between economic growth and low inflation in order to promote monetary stability, the other deficit member countries were forced to trade off economic growth and exchange rate stability (Ferri, 1990, p.6). Given the narrow margins of exchange rate divergence imposed by the EMS agreement, the scope for exchange rate adjustment by the deficit countries was quite limited. Consequently, most of the ERM countries have adopted a "strong currency" option by aligning themselves with the anti-inflationary strategy of the Bundesbank. Although this strategy has fostered greater exchange rate cohesion and discipline within the EMS, evident by the gradual convergence of national inflation rates, the ultimate cost has been the legacy of relatively low levels of economic growth and high rates of cyclical unemployment. Disinflationary policies thus contributed to the onset of "Eurosclerosis" during the 1980s. By 1986, the average unemployment rate in the Community had increased from 4.7 per cent in 1975-80 to around 11 per cent. On the other hand, the rate of inflation had fallen from an average of 12 per cent to 3.7 per cent over the same period (Guerrieri, et al, 1989, p.2).

In terms of the second constraint, the inability of German finance capital to become the centre of payments for the EMS as a whole appears to be closely linked to the structural relationship between German finance and industry. These links which express themselves in the form of interlocking directorships and cross-ownership, prevent the internationalisation of German finance capital. In other words, German finance capital does not exhibit the degree of autonomy that one associates with the London and New York capital markets. The German financial system is therefore driven by the imperatives of industrial capital and the logic of maintaining German export competitiveness. In this sense, the EMS has provided a greater degree of stability in its real effective exchange rate in relation to the US dollar which contributed to the maintenance of Germany's export competitiveness. German exports are concentrated mostly in the capital goods and manufacturing sectors which account for almost two thirds of total exports, while one quarter of the economy is devoted to the export sector which employs over a third of German workers. In order to counteract an appreciating exchange rate in relation to markets outside the Community, the German authorities have pursued a rigorous anti-inflationary strategy which has, more or less, offset any short-term loss of export competitiveness caused by a rise in the nominal exchange rate.

Within Europe, however, the maintenance of exchange rate stability through the Exchange Rate Mechanism has contributed to the promotion of German exports which enjoy an oligopolistic advantage. German exports in Europe tend to exhibit a low degree of price elasticity. At the same time, the accumulation of trade surpluses has had the effect of increasing the share of profits in the economy as a whole. Since the increase in the profit share has not necessarily been at the expense of the wages share, redistributional struggles between capital and labour have been either averted or moderated (Kalecki, 1971). It would be plausible to contend that this export-driven logic of the German economy has underpinned its "social market" policies.

The accumulation of structural surpluses in Germany can thus be explained largely by the composition of its exports in finished manufactured goods which enjoy an oligopolistic advantage in the European market. In order to maintain their dominant share of these markets, intra-EC exchange rate cohesion is necessary. From the standpoint of extra-EC exports from Germany, any loss of competitiveness through a nominal exchange rate appreciation has been compensated by a superior anti-inflationary performance. A high nominal exchange rate also tends to encourage the process of industrial restructuring and technological re-conversion through an increase in the capital/output ratio. The EMS has thus provided a relatively stable monetary zone to which a significant share of their exports are destined, while fortifying the German economy from the destabilising impact of a volatile US dollar. At the same time, the threat of competition from Germany's European trade rivals can be effectively countered through the ERM which prevents sudden, sharp devaluations of intra-ERM exchange rates. By anchoring these currencies to the DM, the German economy can maintain its share of exports and continue to enjoy trade surpluses. The growth of German exports, in turn, generates the export of capital. Historically, surplus countries become financial centres by virtue of the inherent stability of their currencies which attracts international demand as a means of payments and as a reserve asset. In the case of Germany, however, this transition has either not yet occurred or has been stifled by the policies of the Bundesbank (Halevi, 1995).

Since the demise of the Bretton Woods system, the Bundesbank has attempted to limit the international role of the DM. This view was motivated primarily by the deep-seated concerns over the excessive creation of liquidity if the DM were to be internationalised. In order to counter the inflationary effect of US expansionary monetary policies, the Bundesbank adopted monetary targeting in 1975. Informed by the prevailing monetarist doctrines which had propounded that monetary growth impacts on the growth of national income, the rate of inflation and the nominal exchange rate, the Bundesbank pursued a low inflationary strategy to induce capital formation. As Table 7.1 highlights, Germany's anti-inflationary record was unrivalled by the major OECD countries. Given this historical credibility, other members of the ERM have chosen to peg their currencies to the German mark in order to acquire similar credentials as stable, low risk countries for investment and long-term capital formation.

Table 7.1 **Comparative Inflation Rates Between the Major OECD Countries; 1970-89**

Period	Germany	US	UK	Japan	France	Italy
1970-74	5.1	6.1	9.6	10.7	7.7	9.1
1975-79	4.2	8.1	15.7	7.5	10.2	15.9
1980-84	4.5	7.5	9.6	3.9	11.2	16.6
1984-89	1.3	3.6	5.3	1.2	3.6	6.2
1970-89	3.9	6.3	10.0	5.8	8.1	11.9

Source: OECD Economic Surveys, 1990.

The unwillingness of the Bundesbank to liberalise financial markets reflected this overriding objective to maintain strict control over monetary growth as the main weapon against inflation. These controls extended to restrictions on foreign bank deposits which were required to have a higher minimum reserve ratio than resident deposits. Capital controls were also imposed on German financial institutions which limited the issuing of DM-denominated bonds in international capital markets. Despite the liberalisation of capital markets in the mid-1980s which abolished most of these restrictions, German capital markets still lag behind the more sophisticated financial centres in London and New York. German capital markets continue to be quite narrow while investment outlets are dominated by the big banks who are reluctant to purchase portfolios of foreign bonds.

In stark contrast, D-mark Eurobonds are bought and sold by investors outside Germany. Indeed, the demand for DM-denominated assets has increased as the process of trade interpenetration has accelerated. Since a growing proportion of this trade is denominated in marks, the demand for DMs has increased. Similarly, the number of German banks operating in foreign countries had risen from only 8 in 1970 to 186 in 1988. Conversely, the number of branches of foreign banks operating in Germany had increased from 25 to 58 over the same period (Tavlas, 1991, pp.19-20). The most striking evidence of the rise in the international role of the DM, however, has been in its use as an intervention currency in the ERM.

Table 7.2   Currency Distribution of Foreign Exchange Intervention (Percentage of the Total; 1979-87)

	Intervention in the EMS		
Currency	1979-82	1983-85	1986-87
US dollars	71.5	53.7	26.3
EMS Currencies	27.2	43.5	71.7
(DMs)	(23.7)	(39.4)	(59.0)
Others	1.3	2.8	2.0

Source: Commission Departments, 1988.

As Table 7.2 demonstrates, the share of US dollar interventions declined from 71.5 per cent in 1979-82 to 26.3 per cent in 1986-87 while the share of DM interventions increased from 23.7 to 59 per cent during the same period. This evidence suggests that the US dollar was gradually replaced by the DM in intra-EMS interventions. After the liberalisation of the German capital markets in 1984-85, the international role of the DM has also increased as a reserve asset and as a means of payments. Between 1980 and 1989, international DM claims in Germany increased by about 180 per cent while those held outside Germany increased by 125 per cent (Tavlas, 1991, p.31).

After the demise of the Bretton Woods system, a three key-currency configuration has emerged with the rise of the DM and the Japanese yen as major reserve currencies. This new configuration reflects the portfolio preferences of investors in their desire to reduce the risks associated with the exclusive use of US dollars and the demand by creditors to diversify away from dollar denominated assets. As the DM appreciated against the US dollar after 1985, long term interest rates reflected this relationship. The fact that German long-term rates were lower than those in the US suggests that the dollar is expected to continue to depreciate. International monetary stability has therefore been increasingly based on the substitution of the three key currencies. While the US dollar has continued to perform the dominant role as an international means of payments, the DM and the yen have emerged as key reserve currencies in international markets by virtue of the fact of their respective trade surpluses. This configuration is only possible as long as international trade remains relatively liberal.

The basic contradiction between growing German trade surpluses and the trade deficits of France and Italy threatened the cohesion and stability of the EMS. Germany's trade surplus with its EMS partners increased more than four-fold between 1979 and 1988. At the same time, France's trade deficit increased more than three-fold (Table 7.3). In other words, German trade surpluses could ultimately generate a vicious circle in Europe as protectionist forces re-emerge on a national level. This spectre has so far been averted because the penetration of German exports has been offset by an increase in German investment in these markets. The refusal of the German authorities to stimulate the level of effective demand, however, has imparted a disinflationary impulse in the EMS zone. There is a very real possibility that a "depressive spiral" could be set in motion as each member state imposes restrictionist policies and tolerates higher levels of unemployment. The "fallacy of composition" would suggest that as each country attempts to increase their exports to other member countries, these exports will be inhibited by the deflationary policies pursued by those countries. If extra-Community markets also diminish, this depressive spiral could degenerate into a vicious circle of competitive devaluations and "beggar thy neighbour" policies. This cumulative process of competitive disinflation has characterised the dynamics of the European economy since the late 1980s (Boltho, 1983).

Table 7.3   Trade Balance of the EMS Countries; 1979-88
$US Billions/(Percentage of GDP)

Country	1979	1983	1986	1987	1988
Belgium	-0.8 (0.7)	-0.8	-0.6	-0.7 (0.5)	-3.4
Denmark	-2.2 (3.4)	-1.1	-3.4	-2.8 (2.9)	-1.8
France	-7.0 (1.2)	-12.4	-17.0	-20.7 (2.3)	-21.9
Germany	5.7 (0.7)	4.1	15.4	22.3 (2.0)	26.5
Ireland	0.3 (8.1)	0.9	1.8	3.0 (24.9)	3.4
Italy	-0.9 (0.3)	-1.3	-3.4	-6.1 (0.8)	-8.6
Netherlands	4.9 (3.1)	10.6	7.3	5.0 (2.3)	5.7

Source: Vona, 1990, p.48.

The extent to which the major deficit countries of France and Italy were willing to tolerate high unemployment by assigning low inflation to the top of their national objectives ultimately determined whether the EMS was able to preserve its internal cohesion. In the absence of a reflationary policy in Germany, the deficit countries had been forced to rely on capital controls to maintain their respective exchange rate parities. This, in turn, compelled the weaker countries to overvalue their currencies which had the effect of distorting their domestic prices and impaired their competitiveness.

The impact of this exchange rate constraint on the ability of a deficit country to pursue an expansionary programme was graphically portrayed in France after the election of the Socialist government in 1981. Within two years, an unprecedented flight of capital had occurred, induced by a two-fold increase in the current account deficit. Over Ff80b had fled the country as the French economy experienced a sudden quadrupling of the national debt from Ff123b in 1980 to Ff451b in 1983 (Petit, 1989, p.259). By early 1983, after the third successive exchange rate crisis, the Mitterand government had abandoned "Keynesianism in one country". Anti-inflationary policies were introduced to stabilise the franc and stem the outflow of capital. In the wake of these measures, the European Commission agreed to provide a loan of 4 billion ECUs to finance the current account deficit.

As the French case demonstrated, the survival of the EMS inevitably depended on the ability of member countries to co-ordinate their macroeconomic policies and to pursue a convergence of national inflation rates. Germany's low inflation has provided an anchor for the other ERM countries while its domestic savings had financed investment in the deficit countries. Conversely, the nominal appreciation of the DM had increased Germany's purchasing power over European assets. During the 1970s, this virtuous circle was based on the configuration of low growth and disinflation in Germany, on the one hand, and high growth and rampant inflation in France and Italy, on the other hand. Consequently, Italy and France experienced an increased penetration of German exports thereby becoming more dependent on German investment. The continuation of this virtuous circle could only be sustained if the deficit countries continued to accommodate German exports. In order to do so, however, the deficit countries were required to make a downward adjustment of their respective exchange rates. During the 1980s, membership of the ERM imposed limits on this exchange rate adjustment. The emphasis was now placed on internal adjustment through a programme of disinflation. By independently targeting its monetary growth, Germany established the inflationary threshold to which its ERM partners aligned themselves. Average inflation in the EMS fell from about 11 per cent in 1980 to around 2 per cent in 1986 while the differentials between the highest and lowest national inflation rates had narrowed from 16 per cent to about 6 per cent (Padoa-Schioppa, 1988, p.371). Figure 7.2 illustrates this convergence of inflation rates.

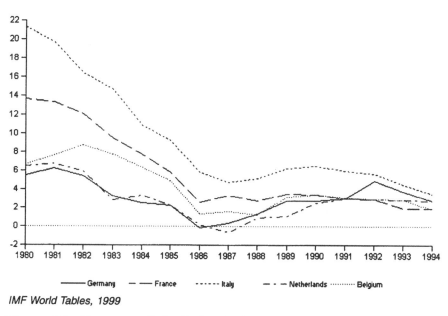

IMF World Tables, 1999

Figure 7.2 **Consumer Price Index (Inflation Rate) in Selected EMS Countries (percentage per annum)**

It should be noted that much of the success of the EMS in terms of the convergence of national inflation rates and exchange rate concertation up until 1989 can be explained largely in the light of the propitious international environment discussed in the previous chapter. The other caveat is that the main burden of adjustment has been borne by the deficit countries in terms of lower growth and higher unemployment. In order to prevent speculative attacks, both France and Italy had imposed more stringent capital controls on the inflow of capital. Figure 7.3 illustrates the relative success in exchange rate concertation up until 1992.

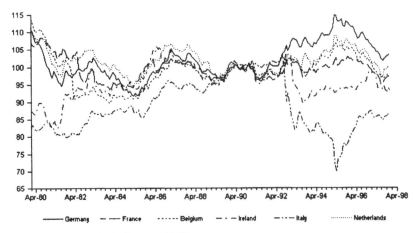

OECD Main Economic Indicators, 1999

Figure 7.3   Real Effective Exchange Rates in Selected EMS Countries (1990=100)

With the signing of the Single European Act (SEA) in 1986, capital controls were scheduled to be abolished in 1992. Consequently, one of the main pillars of the EMS which contributed to the stabilisation of intra-Community exchange rates had disappeared. The liberalisation of capital movements, however, became difficult to reconcile with the continued existence of national exchange rate regimes. This glaring dichotomy became evident during the speculative turmoil that engulfed the EMS in mid-1992. The only solution to this dichotomy appears to be the realisation of complete monetary union which would assimilate the process of money and credit creation on a supranational level with the formation of a European central bank issuing a single currency. Monetary union implies a symmetrical regime of exchange rate concertation. The EMS, however, had been characterised by asymmetrical exchange rate relations with Germany acting as the nominal exchange rate anchor for the system as a whole. It is precisely this crucial issue which will determine the ultimate outcome of the EMU experiment. In other words, to what extent will the demands of the German monetary authorities impinge on the process of monetary union in

Europe? Or to pose the question in a different guise: will the Bundesbank be willing to surrender its monetary autonomy? The whole issue therefore reverts to the political ramifications of German economic hegemony.

II. A Single Currency?

The Brussels Council which had established the EMS in 1978 had identified the ECU as the pivot around which intra-EMS exchange rates would be expressed. The ECU would constitute the official numeraire for the ERM and the means of settlement between the central banks. From these quite modest foundations, it was envisaged that the ECU would eventually evolve into a single currency. However, the ECU was devoid of legal tender status and restrictions were imposed on its convertibility. According to Masera (1987), the limited role of official ECUs as a means of payments, had stemmed from the reluctance of central banks, most notably the Bundesbank, to undertake "symmetrical" interventions which would adversely affect their monetary bases. In other words, compulsory interventions at the margins through the VSTF were governed by central bank swap agreements which generated the movement of reserves in both directions. This implied a contraction of the monetary bases of the weak currency countries and an expansion of the intervening strong currency countries. Unless these capital inflows are sterilised by the central bank of the latter, the growth of liquidity could induce an increase in inflation. As a result, most central bank interventions were voluntary and intra-marginal to prevent currency fluctuations from reaching their compulsory divergence thresholds. Quite contrary to the original EMS agreement, intra-marginal and asymmetrical interventions have predominated.

> It should be noted here that in the asymmetrical arrangement the flow of liquidity from the periphery to the centre country does not affect the money stock in the latter country. In this asymmetrical system, the centre country automatically sterilises the liquidity inflow by reverse open market operations. If it did not do so, the monetary expansion engineered by the peripheral country would lead to an increase of the money stock of the centre country. That country would then also lose its function of an anchor for the whole system (De Grawe, 1992, p.118).

Despite the limited use of official ECUs in the financing and intervention mechanisms of the EMS, the growth of private ECUs had been quite substantial. Since the process of credit creation occurred through the mechanism of the VSTF in which the participating countries of the ERM are compelled to intervene at the margins by borrowing ECUs in unlimited amounts, the growth of secondary ECUs were created by the stock of primary ECUs through the revolving swap agreements between central banks. These primary ECUs were issued in exchange for the deposit of twenty per cent of the gold and dollar reserves by the central banks with the EMCF. A rudimentary reserve structure was thus established for the expansion of official ECUs. Table 7.4 illustrates this reserve composition of the EMS between 1979 and 1985.

Table 7.4   Net Official Reserves of Countries in the ERM
(\$US Billions)

	1979	1982	1985
Gold	77.5	86.9	80.0
Convertible Currencies	55.0	36.9	58.5
(dollars)	(50.0)	(30.6)	(37.3)
(EMS Currencies)	(4.3)	(4.4)	(17.4)
ECUs	38.2	37.6	35.2
Net position on:			
The IMF	10.4	11.4	12.0
Others	-6.3	-14.6	-12.1
Total	174.8	158.2	173.6

Source: Micossi, p.333.

By 1985, private ECUs accounted for about 3 per cent of the international currency market and had risen to fifth rank in terms of the denomination of foreign bond issues (Masera, 1987, p.11). Most of this expansion was attributed to Italian and French private agents and public enterprises attracted by the lower risk premium and lower interest rates offered by ECU-denominated borrowings. The expansion of ECU-bonds, however, only accounted for a negligible proportion of the total borrowings within the Community. In early 1985, the Committee of Central Bank Governors agreed to ease some of the restrictions imposed on official ECUs by allowing central banks outside the EMS to purchase ECUs. These operations, however, were presided over by the BIS and confined to temporary swap agreements. International demand for Ecus had increased which improved the liquidity of these financial instruments and enhanced their role as an international reserve asset. This trend was reflected in the increase in the share of total ECU issues made by foreign borrowers from about 10 per cent to 40 per cent between 1982 and 1985 (Micossi, 1985, pp.339-40).

The rise of private Ecus in international markets appears to coincide with the "parallel currency" proposals of the "All Saints Day" manifesto announced by a group of nine prominent economists as early as November 1975 (Economist, 1/11/75). According to this manifesto, a single currency - the Europa - would circulate in direct competition with the existing plethora of national currencies. The market would ultimately determine if the Europa would supersede the existing system of national currencies. A similar proposal for a parallel currency was promoted by the British alternative plan to the Delors Report in 1989 but failed to attract Community support (George, 1991, p.183). Given the inconvertibility of the ECU and its primary function as a unit of account in central bank operations, its potential status as a European currency was constrained by the absence of a European central bank.

A single European currency would doubtless foster a more equitable sharing of the burden of exchange rate adjustment between Member States. In theory, a single currency would provide a more efficient means of central bank intervention. By circumventing the dollar/DM relationship which lies at the very heart of asymmetrical, intra-EMS exchange rate relations, monetary union would abolish the speculative propensities caused by short-term shifts in portfolio holdings of existing national currencies. Despite these compelling economic arguments in favour of monetary union, the greatest obstacle remains the reluctance of the Bundesbank to surrender its sovereignty over monetary policies. In order to attract the support of the Bundesbank, the ECB would need to mirror the policies and structure of the former. In other words, price stability would have to be assigned as the paramount objective of the ECB, while the ECB Board would need to exhibit political independence.

These German objectives, however, have encountered French opposition. The French have been strident advocates of political control over monetary policy. In the course of the Council of Ministers meeting in Dublin in December 1996, the French proposal that growth as well as price stability should be enshrined as an objective of EMU monetary policy was successfully endorsed. The meeting established a new Ministerial "stability council" as a political counterweight to the ECB. Similarly, at the European

Summit in Amsterdam in June 1997, the newly elected Socialist government of Jospin endorsed an employment chapter to the Maastricht Treaty which elevated employment as a parallel goal to price stability (Feldstein, 1997). As EMU evolves, there exists the potential for serious conflict over the political objectives of monetary policy. These divisions appear to echo the "economist/monetarist" debates of the early 1970s.

Conclusion

The implications of German economic hegemony manifest themselves in the asymmetrical dynamics of intra-European trade and exchange rate relations. The emergence of Germany as the dominant core country of the European economy was mirrored in the concomitant rise of the DM as the nominal exchange rate anchor for the European Monetary System. Given the German ideological preference for a low inflationary strategy, a cumulative process of competitive disinflation between ERM Member States was set in motion as each country attempted to emulate the German preference for low inflationary growth. Unlike Germany, however, the weaker deficit countries could not accomplish a trade-off between economic growth and low inflation in order to promote exchange rate stability. This exchange rate constraint only accentuated the powerful disinflationary forces within the EMS zone and contributed to an increase in unemployment. Consequently, the process of "competitive disinflation" threatened to induce a vicious circle as each country was compelled to adopt an export-led strategy of growth in order to overcome their respective balance of payments deficit. As each country implemented policies which dampened the level of effective demand, however, the propensity to import was curtailed. The spectre of a "depressive spiral" was averted because German trade surpluses were accompanied by an increase in German investment in the EMS zone. Furthermore, the economic recovery of the US economy provided an expanding market for European exports.

While Germany increased its export surpluses within the EMS zone, Italy and France, in particular, experienced an increase in their respective trade deficits with Germany. This asymmetrical trade configuration could ultimately threaten the stability and cohesion of the EMS. In the absence of a German policy of reflation, the deficit countries experienced higher levels of unemployment. In theory, monetary union should ease these asymmetrical tensions by imposing a more equitable sharing of the burden of structural adjustment. With the emergence of German economic dominance, however, it would be reasonable to contend that the institutional framework will tend to reflect German ideological preferences. Indeed, the ratification of the Maastricht Treaty in 1993 suggests that the strategy to achieve monetary union has already assimilated the monetarist paradigm favoured by Germany and enshrined in the strict convergence criteria imposed on countries in order to qualify for membership.[3]

---

3   This issue will be discussed at greater length in Chapter 9.

PART III
THE INTERNAL
MARKET PROGRAMME

8 Project 1992

Introduction

In the aftermath of the second oil price shocks of 1978-79, the economies of the EC-12 experienced the most severe recession since the reconversion crisis of 1947-48. Although the recession was international in its scope, the performance of the EC-12 was worse than in the US and Japan. Within five years, unemployment had doubled. Indeed, since the mid-1970s, the phenomena of what was euphemistically referred to as the onset of "Eurosclerosis" - the combination of high unemployment and low economic growth - had pervaded the economic landscape. Between 1974 and 1985, the economies of the EC-12 had been outperformed by their international rivals in Japan and the United States. While Community economic growth had averaged only 1.9 per cent each year during this period, the US and Japan had experienced an average of 2.4 and 3.8 per cent respectively. Similarly, inflation in the EC-12 stood at an average of 11 per cent compared with 7 per cent in the US and 6.3 per cent in Japan over the same period. The relative economic performance of the EC-12 between 1974 and 1990 is highlighted in Table 8.1.

Table 8.1   Comparative International Economic Indicators; 1974-90

	1974-79	1980-85	1986-90
EC-12 (a)	2.5	1.4	3.1
(b)	4.8	9.2	9.9
(c)	12.3	9.8	4.4
US (a)	2.4	2.4	3.0
(b)	6.7	8.0	5.8
(c)	8.5	6.7	4.0
Japan (a)	3.6	3.7	4.6
(b)	1.9	2.4	2.5
(c)	9.9	3.6	1.3
Total OECD (a)	2.7	2.8	2.7
(b)	5.1	7.5	7.1
(c)	10.5	8.3	4.8

(a) Growth Rates
(b) Unemployment Rates
(c) Inflation

Source: OECD Economic Indicators, 1992.

Between 1973 and 1985, intra-Community trade had stagnated and had declined in some sectors. The trade-creating dynamics of the Common Market had therefore ceased to provide a catalyst in the process of economic integration. To be sure, with the decline in the volume of world trade after the first oil price shocks, the European Customs Union had begun to resemble the caricature portrayed by its critics as "fortress Europe". Trade diversion had increasingly defined its behaviour. The crisis of excess capacity in the shipbuilding, steel, textile and car industries had culminated in the imposition of import quotas, state aid and indirect tariff restrictions by national governments which threatened to develop into destructive intra-EC trade wars. Quite apart from these visible forms of protectionism, "non-tariff" barriers continued to proliferate. The most common of these barriers were the plethora of selective policies of government procurement which would favour domestic firms at the expense of foreign competitors. According to Padoa-Schioppa, government procurement (excluding military expenditure) was estimated to have accounted for almost 200 billion ECUs per year or equivalent to about 6 per cent of the Community GDP (Padoa-Schioppa, 1987, p.34).

The causes of this crisis were the subject of perennial debates centred around the structural weaknesses of Europe's industry and the growing perception that the continent had fallen behind their competitors in their traditional markets and in the strategic high technology sectors. This was reflected most strikingly in the increased penetration of European markets by American and Japanese transnational corporations in the automobile and electronics sectors. Confronted by the globalisation of production and an intensification of competitive forces, European firms were impelled to rationalise and restructure their operations. The creation of a unified European "home" market was therefore perceived as a necessary condition by which to re-launch a new phase of capital accumulation. In order to reverse this process of economic stagnation, the Internal Market Programme emerged as a neo-liberal solution in which all of the existing barriers to the free movement of labour, capital, goods and services would be abolished by 1992.

I. The Neo Liberal Ascendancy

The neo-liberal ascendancy was reflected in a general shift to political right within the EC during the 1980s, regardless of the ideological persuasion of the respective political parties in power. This was most evident in France after the abandonment of "Keynesianism in one country" by the Socialist government in 1983. Similarly, the Spanish Socialists pursued free market policies after their election in 1981. Given this political configuration, the Thatcher government in the UK found it quite propitious to support the single market proposals despite opposition to institutional and procedural reforms embodied by the principle of majority voting in the Council of Ministers and the European Social Charter. The political agenda of the Community was therefore dominated by the governments in power in the northern industrial "core" countries of France, Germany and the UK. This favourable political configuration made it possible for a recasting of the European bargain towards a neo-liberal direction (Grahl & Teague, 1989).

From the standpoint of the neo-liberal paradigm, the prevailing national regimes of accumulation had exhausted themselves. The crisis of overcapacity and economic stagnation had exposed the limits of these national strategies which had been governed by the "social market" policies of both the Christian Democrats and Social Democratic coalitions. Neo-liberal critics argued that these national policies could no longer be legitimised. This paradigm shift away from the prevailing corporatist forms of State regulation (ie, the welfare state, Keynesianism and industry intervention) coincided with the demands of transnational corporations based in Europe that these national modes of regulation and protectionism should be gradually abolished. National deregulation, privatisation of public corporations and market liberalisation became the neo-liberal mantra. The removal of non-tariff barriers, the opening up of public procurement policies and liberalisation of capital markets also conformed with these transnational objectives. Most of these ostensible "efficiency" gains would be secured through cost reductions and rationalisation in order to promote greater economies of scale and improve competitiveness. The neo-Liberal strategy not only implied the dismantling of national modes of regulation but the curbing of the power of organised labour in order to foster greater labour market flexibility and mobility.

Even before the official ratification of the Single European Act (SEA), European big business had been mobilising support in the European Commission to adopt a neo-liberal solution to the lack of economic dynamism and growth. These demands coalesced in the Roundtable of European Industrialists, an organisation represented by Europe's most powerful corporations, including Phillips, Siemens, Olivetti, Fiat, GEC, Daimler Benz, Volvo, ASEA, Bosch and Ciba-Geigy. One of the architects of this elite group was the Commissioner for Industry, Etienne Davignon. An elite alliance soon emerged between transnational business interests and the European Commission which culminated in the election of Delors to the Presidency of the Commission in early 1985 (Moravcsik, 1991).

The process of inter-State bargaining over the proposals of the SEA was launched during the European Council Summit at Fontainbleau in June 1984. From this Summit, the Doogue Committee was established and chaired by Lord Cockfield who was the British Commissioner for Trade and Industry. It was from this Committee that the final SEA White Paper entitled "The Completion of the Internal Market" was presented to the Council at the Luxembourg Summit in March 1985 (George, 1991, p.160). A few months later in Brussels, the Council agreed to a timetable for the 279 proposals to be implemented by December, 1992. By the end of the year, the SEA was officially ratified by the Council and signed by the twelve Member States in February 1986. The legislation eventually came into legal force in July 1987 after referenda were held in Denmark and Ireland (Tsoukalis, 1993, p.61).

The SEA defines the single market as "an area without internal barriers in which the free movement of goods, persons, services and capital is ensured" (Article 8a). In order to realise these objectives, however, a revision of the Rome Treaty was necessary in four spheres:

1. Legislation to simplify the process of harmonisation to essential standards even though mutual recognition of divergent laws and regulations would continue to exist in accordance to the principle of subsidiarity.
2. The introduction of majority voting in the Council.
3. An increase in the legislative powers of the parliament in order to redress the "democratic deficit" of the Community.
4. The promotion of economic and monetary integration through a strategy of "parallelism" which would involve:
   - The realisation of complete monetary union.
   - The harmonisation of social policies in relation to minimum wages, working conditions and social welfare policies.
   - The promotion of Community projects in scientific and technological spheres.
   - Uniform environmental protection laws.
   - The closer co-ordination of national fiscal policies.

The process of economic and legal harmonisation would be accompanied by the introduction of majority voting in the Council of Ministers (Article 100a) in order to allow the passage of the SEA legislation to be adopted more easily. The only exceptions involved agreements over capital liberalisation and treaties governing air and sea transport. Consequently, the SEA linked the liberalisation of the internal market with procedural reform. The famous Luxembourg Compromise of 1967 which had enshrined the powers of national veto over Community legislation was temporarily suspended. Community constitutional and legal prerogatives, however, were merely confined to legislation related to the SEA. In this crucial sense, the SEA embraced a much wider agenda to include increased powers of the European parliament, social cohesion and collaboration in research and development. The Social Action Programme involved over fifty measures which cover the free movement of labour within the Community, the basic wage, training and associated health, safety and other working conditions. Although the structural funds were doubled, the Social Charter encountered quite trenchant opposition from the Thatcher government which regarded these proposals as ideological anathema.

The initiative for political reform originated from the "Crocodile Club" which was composed of the most prominent supporters of the federalist cause. One of its leaders, Altierio Spinelli, was instrumental in formulating the resolution in the European parliament which established the draft treaty for European political union as early as July 1981. The draft treaty was adopted by an overwhelming majority of the EP in February 1984. One of the central pillars was the principle of "subsidiarity" which informed the Maastricht Treaty in 1992. In other words, common action between Member States would require a majority vote whereas unanimity would apply to the more sensitive political agreements (Wistrich, 1989, pp.38-39).

At the Milan Summit meeting in June 1985, an intergovernmental conference was established to discuss political and procedural reforms. These discussions culminated in the procedural reforms embodied in the SEA. The EP would be given greater legislative powers to amend Council proposals. If the EP's amendments were accepted by the Commission, then the Council could only reject these amendments by a unanimous vote whereas only a majority vote was required by the Council to accept these amendments (Daltrop, 1992, p.91). Similarly, the application for EC membership and association agreements with third countries were now subject to parliamentary approval (Wistrich, 1989, p.9). Although the executive powers of the Council of Ministers remained intact, these procedural reforms signalled a willingness to increase the legislative powers of the EP. The SEA also enshrined formal legal status to the European Political Co-operation (EPC) in the formulation of a common foreign policy and the informal summit meetings between the twelve European government leaders (Nugent, 1991, p.36).

The neo-liberal strategy was therefore accompanied by a set of policy-led initiatives. Despite British opposition, Delors had sought to complement these deregulatory measures on the national level with new forms of regulation on the supranational level. The application of "competition among rules" governed these policy initiatives (Woolcock, et al, 1991, p.9). Delors' vision encompassed a European "organised space" between the nation-state and the global market. In other words, Europe would become the organising centre of a regional regulatory bloc to counter the destabilising forces of globalisation (Ross, 1992, p.62). The neo-liberal strategy was informed by the overwhelming imperative to improve Europe's competitiveness in the global market. With the publication of the influential Cecchini Report in 1988, a blueprint for this strategy had been sketched out.

According to the Cecchini Report, the economic benefits of the SEA were estimated at about 6 per cent of the Community GDP (Cecchini, 1988). In retrospect, these estimates were quite optimistic. The more heroic assumptions could be identified with the neo-liberal faith in the efficacy of the market. The basic theoretical contention was that market liberalisation would hasten the Schumpeterian dynamic of "creative destruction" and generate an increase in the level of productive investment and economic restructuring through the purgative forces induced by competition. Moreover these competitive forces would ostensibly foster a rapid upsurge in the rate of corporate mergers and promote greater economies of scale and increased returns to scale as firms integrated their operations across national borders. The whole strategy hinged on the dismantling of national forms of capitalist regulation and state support for "national champions". The fatal flaw of the neo-liberal programme, however, was the absence of corresponding regimes of regulation on the supranational level. This was especially evident in the relatively minor role performed by the EC budget as a redistributive mechanism and the very limited development of coherent Community state structures and apparatuses.

The Single Market Programme also reflected dramatic changes in international geo-political alignments. With the relative demise of the post-war system of *Pax Americana,* the single market emerged as a regional organising centre of the emergent tripolar system of economic blocs. This redivision of the world market was accompanied by the disintegration of the Soviet bloc. As a result of these dramatic post-Cold War re-alignments, the Community's international relations have been transformed beyond recognition. In contrast to its former role as a strategic bulwark against the Soviet Union, the Community became the new focus or "centre" to which the newly emergent capitalist countries of eastern Europe gravitated toward. After the collapse of the Soviet bloc in 1989, the US defense umbrella of NATO had lost its *raison d'etre.* A more independent defence and foreign policy was now possible.

After German re-unification, support for closer European co-operation was perceived as a necessary corollary in order to assimilate the former East German socialist State. At the same time, the prospect of potential export markets and investment in eastern Europe had rekindled Germany's traditional economic dominance of this region (Spaulding,

1991). In this sense, the former socialist countries could now emerge as possible candidates for EC membership. The existing EC-12 have thus evolved as the core of a system of concentric circles with the EFTA countries and the former socialist countries gravitating as satellite states around this "core". The EFTA countries have signed agreements to establish a European Economic Area which requires them to adhere to EC rules and procedures even though formal membership is still in its transitional phase. At the Edinburgh European Council in December 1992 it was agreed to proceed with enlargement negotiations with Austria, Norway and Sweden (Artis & Lee, 1994, p.29). The former socialist countries, on the other hand, have negotiated association agreements with the Community in 1991 (Ross, 1992). These were designed to align eastern Europe with the Community's economic and institutional procedures and norms.

Although the Franco-German accord continued to govern the political dynamics of the pan-European project, the inter-State bargaining process had been modified substantially with the engagement of the UK and the other new Member States. Both Kohl and Mitterand viewed Project 1992 as a catalyst in revitalising the European project after more than a decade of stagnation and political inertia. Indeed, the political timing proved to be almost uncanny since it coincided with an economic resurgence in the late 1980s. As the mini-boom gained momentum, the political climate changed from one of a pervasive "Europessimism" to an excessive optimism. The euphoria became self-fulfilling. Despite the Thatcher government's opposition to elements of procedural reform embodied in the SEA, the perennial disputes over British financial contributions to the EC budget and ideological opposition to the Social Charter, support for the SEA was assured by the potential benefits that British financial institutions could derive with the liberalisation of financial markets. Thatcher's Gaullist tactics failed to have any lasting impact on the momentum generated by the Commission. It was the dynamism of the Commission, led by the skilful political talents of Delors which provided a new impetus in the revival of the neo-functionalist "snow-ball" effect.

II. A European Social Space?

Given the prevailing doctrines of "negative integration" which had informed the Rome treaties and the subsequent evolution of the Common Market, social policies have only played a minor role in the formulation of

Community strategies. Much of the earlier social legislation was inherited from the ECSC (Article 56) which involved the creation of a Social Fund on a 50-50 basis with national governments to assist in the resettlement of workers from declining industrial regions and contribute to education and re-training (Shanks, 1977). Social policy is enshrined in Articles 117 and 118 of the Treaty of Rome. While Articles 117-118 relate to the agreements by Member States to improve working conditions, Articles 123-28 provide the statutory basis for the Social Fund (Artis, et al, p.282). Furthermore, the freedom of movement of labour within the customs union constitutes one of the main pillars of the Treaty. These provisions are enshrined in Articles 48-58 of the Rome Treaty (Tsoukalis, 1993, p.150).

In the course of the negotiations over the first enlargement at the Hague Summit in 1969, social policy was conferred a more prominent status. This culminated in the Social Action Programme adopted in 1974 which comprised a rather incoherent and disparate set of policies to promote employment in the more depressed regions, worker participation in management decisions and greater consultation with the Social and Economic Committees of the Community. These measures, however, were condemned to have very little impact in the face of rising unemployment and the constraints imposed by national governments. The shortage of funds and the unwillingness of national governments to transfer resources to the Community for these programmes prevented the formulation of a more coherent social policy. Social policy continued to be informed by the principles of negative integration and the prevailing liberal strategies which focused on the priorities of the free movement of labour and the equalisation of competitive conditions between enterprises within the customs union (Shanks, 1977, p.13).

With the second enlargement of Greece and the Iberian peninsular during the 1980s, social policy was once again given a new impetus. By 1986 about 7 per cent of the Community budget was devoted to the Social Fund which represented a five fold increase over the previous decade (Wistrich, 1989, p.69). In May 1989 the Commission produced the first draft of a Social Charter as part of the Internal Market Programme. Despite some modifications and a dilution of its social objectives in the face of British opposition, the second draft failed to reverse these trenchant British objections. Delors had identified three main areas in the creation of a European "social space": (1) a charter of social rights, (2) statutory obligations for workers' participation in management and (3) fostering a dialogue between capital and labour on a European level (Tsoukalis, 1993, p.156). This progressive vision encountered hostile British Tory opposition. The eventual outcome witnessed an unprecedented scenario in which the other eleven Member States signed a separate social protocol at the Strasbourg Summit in December 1989. The Social Charter formed the basis of the Social Chapter of the Maastricht Treaty signed in December 1991 and ratified by all of the Member States, with the exception of Britain, in 1993. Under Article 118 of this Treaty, the Community can legislate by a qualified majority vote on issues of health and safety, employment conditions and equal employment opportunity principles. Unanimity, however, is required for legislation covering worker participation, social security and the social protection of workers (Tsoukalis, 1993, p.172).

European trade unions, represented by the European Trade Union Confederation (ETUC), had quite legitimate reservations about the social consequences of the neo-liberal strategy. Their greatest concern was the possible emergence of "social dumping" in the event of the removal of barriers on intra-European investment and competition. There was an explicit danger that firms would exploit lower wages and working conditions in the less developed regions in order to undermine established wages, conditions and fundamental labour rights in the Community as a whole. It was in this context that the first draft of the Social Charter had sought to harmonise wages and social security provisions across the EC. Confronted by hostile British opposition, however, the proposals were diluted and became a mere statement of intent, devoid of any real legislative imperatives (George, 1991, p.207).

As a result of British opposition, the Social Charter was largely symbolic. Articles 100a and 118a of the SEA enshrine legislation to improve and harmonise national standards of health and safety, environmental laws and consumer protection. The need to compensate those regions and social groups that would be adversely affected by economic restructuring was enshrined in Articles 130a and 130b of the SEA which commits the EC to strengthen social cohesion through the regional and structural funds, including the Social Fund. Beyond these measures, it is evident that the neo-liberal strategy has prevailed by confining the social dimension of the Internal Market Programme to the issues of labour mobility and minimal regulation on a European level. The final draft of the Social Charter was devoid of any legal force and had become nothing more than an act of symbolism.

Conclusion

The restoration of the competitive dynamism of European capitalism through the purgative forces generated by the neo-liberal strategy cannot be taken for granted. Throughout the history of capitalism, the role of the State has been pre-eminent in regulating and mediating between competing class and sectoral interests (McEachern, 1990). Whether this role corresponds with the nation-state or with supranational forms of regulation, the State provides an essential means by which to counter market failure and manage the business cycle through traditional Keynesian policies. The neo-liberal strategy threatens to abolish existing national regimes of accumulation and modes of regulation without producing a coherent regulatory regime on the supranational level. Consequently, with the development of European based MNCs in the global market, the crucial issue of "territorial non-coincidence" will manifest itself. Confronted by an intensification of global oligopolistic competition, European firms could resort to protectionist demands from their respective national governments. The whole dilemma therefore reduces itself to the basic contradiction between the existing national regimes of accumulation, on the one hand, and the growing demands of European MNCs to decompose these structures and create a unified European "domestic" market.

Project 1992 was imbued with the nostalgia of the 1950s. In order to resolve fundamental structural weaknesses, the liberal economic paradigm was re-invented (Milward, 1992, pp.441-442). This was accomplished in the background of momentous historical events in the former Soviet bloc. In this post-Cold War era, the emergence of a regulated economic bloc in Europe represents the more advanced expression of a new tri-polar world system of economic relations. In this schema, the United States under the umbrella of NAFTA and Japan/East Asia constitute the other two poles of capital accumulation. The objective historical conditions by which these economic blocs evolve will determine whether they assume either an exclusive/protectionist form on the one hand, or a more open and liberal regime, on the other hand. From this perspective, Delors' vision of a European "organised space" marks an important historical watershed in the evolution of the single market in Europe.

9 The Maastricht Blueprint for EMU

Introduction

The Maastricht Treaty represents the crowning of the edifice of the Single European Act (SEA). Despite its turbulent and difficult passage, the treaty was finally ratified by Member States, with the exception of Denmark, in January 1993. The treaty embodies a revision of the Rome treaties and enshrines the objective of monetary union in the Community's protocols and principles. The two central tenets of the Treaty are informed by the principles of "subsidiarity" and "parallelism". Subsidiarity simply states that those economic policy functions which can be more effectively enacted by the Community should be transferred from the national level. Parallelism refers to a balance in the Community's economic policies between the three main branches of public policy - allocation, stabilisation and redistribution - in order to promote greater economic integration and cohesion. The most innovative aspect of the treaty is the protocol on the Statute of the European System of Central Banks (ESCB) which enshrines the objective of monetary union.

In June 1988 the European Council meeting in Hanover established the Committee for the Study of Economic and Monetary Union under the chairmanship of Delors. The Delors Report, submitted in April 1989 and ratified by the Member States at the Rome Summit in October 1990, provided the blueprint for monetary union. There were many close similarities with the Werner Report of the early 1970s, most notably in the liberalisation of capital markets, the irrevocable locking of exchange rates, the centralisation of monetary policy and the creation of a single European currency. The Delors plan viewed the existing EMS architecture as the institutional foundation for the completion of the monetary edifice.

In this chapter, the strategy adopted by the Maastricht Treaty will be critically analysed. The focus will be on the efficacy of the "convergence criteria" imposed on Member States in order to qualify for membership of the final phase of EMU. The economic ramifications of this process of "competitive disinflation" will be highlighted to reveal its impact on the weaker deficit countries. Similarly, the issue of fiscal federalism will also be discussed to assess the ability of this supranational regime to perform the economic functions of re-distribution and stabilisation.

I. The Delors Plan

The Maastricht Treaty established a formal timetable for the progressive stages set out by the Delors Report toward EMU. The treaty also identified and elaborated on the "convergence criteria" required to qualify for membership of the final phase and the charter for a European Central Bank (ECB). Monetary union would be accomplished through three progressive stages. During the first stage which officially began on July 1 1990, the EMS Member States were scheduled to abolish all existing capital controls on the movement of capital across national borders. In order to prevent a speculative attack, the degree of exchange rate concertation and surveillance between central banks was strengthened. In December 1991 an agreement to establish the ECB was ratified even though exchange rate re-alignments were still permitted. The second stage was launched on January 1 1994 with the creation of the European Monetary Institute (EMI) which has prepared the groundwork for a more cohesive regime of central bank co-ordination. However, the EMI was not assigned any real powers to act as a de facto central bank but has merely monitored progress on the convergence criteria during the transitional phase leading up to complete monetary union. The final phase would depend on progress achieved by the Member States in conforming to the convergence criteria. If these conditions were satisfied, the final stage was scheduled to begin at the end of 1996. With the onset of the currency turmoil of 1992, however, the final stage has been scheduled to begin on January 1 1999 by those countries that qualify for membership (Appendix A).

The famous "convergence criteria" can be summarised as follows:

1. *The national inflation rate not to exceed 1.5 per cent of the best performing member.*

2. *Budget deficits to be reduced to 3 per cent of GDP and the public debt not to exceed 60 per cent of GDP.*

3. *The exchange rate to remain within the narrow band of 2.25 per cent for two years before admission to the final stage.*

4. *Interest rate differentials to be narrowed within 2 per cent of the lowest national rates.*

A certain degree of discretion and flexibility is possible in the interpretation of a country's attainment of these targets. In other words, caveats are provided. The fiscal criteria, in particular, are subject to a considerable degree of discretion (Article 104c). If the level of a country's primary public debt ratio is declining and approaching the reference value, then the excess can be disregarded. Indeed, after the signing of the Maastricht Treaty, only France and Luxembourg had fulfilled these targets on public debt. The re-unification of Germany had caused an inflationary upsurge and a burgeoning fiscal deficit. At the same time, Spain and the UK had joined the EMS in October 1990 within the wider six per cent band.

From the very outset of the Delors Plan, three major groups of countries could be identified. First there was the original core group under the narrow 2.25 per cent margin of exchange rate fluctuation which had exhibited the lowest rates of inflation. The second group were the high inflation/high public debt countries of Italy, the UK, Spain and Ireland which had adopted the 6 per cent band of the ERM. Finally, there was the third group of less industrialised countries of Greece and Portugal which remained outside the ERM. Given this extreme divergence in economic attributes between individual countries, a "two-speed" Europe evolved with the northern industrial core countries of Germany, the Netherlands, France and the former EFTA countries, on the one hand, and the high inflation/deficit countries of Spain, Portugal, Ireland, Greece and Italy, on the other hand. In institutional terms, the emergence of a "two speed" Europe is embodied in Article 109J (paragraph 4) which states that the final stage of EMU will begin by January 1 1999 regardless of whether the majority of Member States conform with the convergence criteria (Goodhardt, 1993, p.221).

The Maastricht Treaty proposes that the ECB should be governed by two fundamental principles. First, the Statutes of the ECB should declare price stability as its overriding objective (Article 103 of the Treaty and Article 2 of the ECB Charter). Second, the ECB Charter should be inscribed with political and institutional independence. Doubtless these protocols exhibit a striking resemblance with the Charter of the Bundesbank. This is also reflected in the structure and organisation of the ECB insofar as both have independent Councils formulating the general parameters of monetary policy which are discharged by their respective Boards. The ECB Council also has the power to define the ECU central rates within the ERM, the conduct of open market operations and a common exchange rate policy in the event of monetary union. In order to perform these functions, the ECB will be provided with funds from the national central banks (Articles 28 and 29) and will accumulate foreign assets and reserves. Consequently, the bank will earn income on its accumulated assets and distribute the revenue to the national central banks according to their respective capital shares (Article 32). This latter provision is intended to ensure that the ECB will preserve its independent status.

There is still considerable ambiguity over responsibility for the conduct of monetary policy. The Maastricht Treaty divided responsibility for exchange rate policy between the ECB and the EU Economics and Finance Council (ECOFIN) which consists of the Cabinet Ministers of Member States. Whereas ECOFIN has been assigned the role of determining the long-term exchange rate, the ECB presides over short-term interest rate policy and nominal, discretionary changes in the Euro exchange rate. Similarly, the ECB will have a Board of six members headed by the President but monetary policy will also be determined in concert with the central bank Governors of the Member States. Quite clearly, there exists considerable potential for conflict over monetary policy as member countries pursue contradictory national aims.[4]

After the final stage of monetary union, the ECB will be conferred with the authority to issue a single currency. The euro will compete against the US dollar and the Japanese yen as an international vehicular currency. According to Emerson, the direct benefits of a single currency will account for about 0.05 per cent of the Community GDP when translated into net savings in intra-EC transaction costs and is estimated to accrue one-time seigniorage gains of about $US35b (Emerson, 1992, p.25). The real benefits, however, are difficult to quantify and will be realised in the form of greater insulation from the adverse impact of US dollar volatility on the terms of trade. Indeed, the creation of a zone of monetary stability has been the guiding principle of the architects of EMU since the demise of the Bretton Woods system in the early 1970s. From a political standpoint EMU

---

4   These tensions have already surfaced over the appointment of the first ECB President. While the Germans supported the appointment of Win Duisenberg - the Dutch central banker and head of the EMI - for the first eight year term, the French nominated their own candidate, Jean-Claude Trichet, the Governor of the Bank of France. The final compromise witnessed the appointment of Duisenberg for the first four years and Trichet for the second four years.

will provide a more coherent and unified voice in international fora and simplify the process of international macroeconomic co-ordination. A common monetary and exchange rate policy will therefore elevate the political and trade profile of the EU and contribute to a more stable multipolar world monetary system.

II. Competitive Disinflation

Possibly the most contentious and politically sensitive aspect of the Maastricht accord involves the technical prohibition of the financing of public deficits by the ECB (Article 21.1 of the ECB Statute). Moreover, the ECB is also prohibited from acting as a "lender of last resort" to a financially bankrupt government, although in theory the ECB can conduct open market operations which might involve the purchase of government debt in secondary markets. In order to prevent the monetisation of public debts, national governments are obliged to maintain low public debt/GDP ratios. This provision of the treaty has important implications for the high deficit members of Italy, Spain, Greece and Portugal; all of whom rely quite extensively on revenue derived through seigniorage. These seigniorage gains are illustrated in Figure 9.1. Given the constraints imposed on the level of public debt, the scope for fiscal expansion to promote employment has been severely limited. In fact, the whole paradigm that informs the Delors Plan appears to be governed by prevailing monetarist economic theories.

The abolition of capital controls also raises quite profound implications for the high deficit countries. Capital market liberalisation will mean a loss of public control over national interest rates which could undermine the ability of ERM countries to maintain exchange rate parities. The choice will be between the imposition of highly restrictive fiscal policies to compensate for the loss of monetary policy instruments or the acceptance of higher margins of exchange rate movements as a means of external adjustment. If exchange rates are irrevocably fixed, the very real likelihood of a speculative capital flight could be provoked. The speculative turmoil in mid-1992 after the British entry into the ERM was the most recent episode of these recurrent phases of currency volatility. In retrospect, capital liberalisation became incompatible with the existing regime of fixed exchange rates. At the same time, German re-unification had induced a rise in domestic interest rates and the appreciation of the German mark. As the DM appreciated, pressure mounted on the British pound and the Italian lira which culminated in their withdrawal in scenes reminiscent of the earlier "snake" debacle. Market perceptions about the inability of the high inflation/deficit countries to maintain their respective nominal exchange rates in the event of capital liberalisation triggered the speculative attack. A series of devaluations were inevitable either because of the self-fulfilling speculative propensities generated by large capital outflows, or by the exhaustion of foreign exchange reserves to defend the exchange rate.

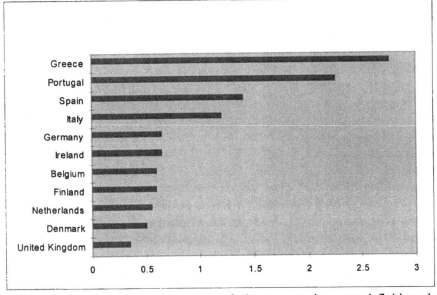

* Seigniorage is calculated in terms of the opportunity cost definition, ie, $s = i * c + (i-ir) * r$ where i is the market short-term interest rate, ir is the interest rate on bank reserves, and c and r are respectively the ratios of currency and bank reserves to GDP.

Source: Emerson, 1992, p.121

Figure 9.1   Seigniorage Revenues in the EC; 1988 (percent of GDP)

The exchange rate crises of mid-1992 were accompanied by the political uncertainty surrounding the ratification of the Maastricht Treaty. In early June, the Danish referendum had rejected the Treaty, while the French referendum held in September had generated considerable uncertainty before it was accepted by a small majority. Despite concerted central bank intervention, the Italian lira and British pound continued to attract speculative attacks. Italy's high level of public debt and budget deficit were perceived by the markets as unsustainable despite the imposition of high real interest rates. Similarly, Britain's high current account deficit and the onset of recession also contributed to the exchange rate crisis as financial markets anticipated a devaluation. By the end of September, British and Italian membership of the ERM were suspended. The successful ratification of the Maastricht Treaty in France and strong German support for the French exchange rate had the effect of dampening these speculative forces. In the course of the speculative crisis, the Italian lira and the British pound had experienced a nominal, effective depreciation of 16 per cent and 15 per cent respectively. The French franc and German mark remained relatively unchanged within the ERM (Blanden-Hovell, 1994, p.342). Over the next year, however, most of the ERM currencies with the exception of the German mark, Dutch guilder and Irish pound, had fallen below their respective divergence threshold which culminated in an increase in the permitted band of exchange rate movement to 15 per cent either side of parity within the ERM in August 1993.

The reverberations of the speculative turmoil of 1992-93 have postponed the EMU timetable for the final stage. With the continued existence of high public debts, similar speculative attacks could be generated in the absence of capital controls. If a country has incurred a large stock of public debt and is faced with an impending fiscal crisis because of its inability to refinance the debt, its credit-worthiness will come under scrutiny by investors and creditors. Financial markets might perceive a reluctance by the authorities to increase interest rates in order to defend the exchange rate because of the adverse effect this would have on the ability of the government to service the debt. Alternatively, the authorities might choose to monetise the public debt through a devaluation, despite the inflationary risks involved. In either case, the conditions are quite propitious for speculative flights and financial panics. The removal of capital controls and the liberalisation of capital markets within a regime of fixed exchange rates therefore incurs quite considerable risks for high inflation/deficit countries as the debacle of 1992-93 has already demonstrated.

The fiscal constraint imposed by the Maastricht Treaty fails to be entirely convincing. Countries that suffer from specific exogenous shocks which temporarily undermines their external balance cannot resort to fiscal stabilisation measures or the imposition of capital controls. They will experience a more painful adjustment with the enactment of a restrictive monetary and fiscal programme. The erosion in the efficacy of national fiscal policies will tend to impart a deflationary bias unless fiscal transfers are augmented on the Community level. However, in its present form, the Community budget is inadequate to perform this function. Similarly, the surrender of monetary policy to a European central bank leaves the national authorities with only the instrument of fiscal policy with which to pursue counter-cyclical and stabilisation measures. In this sense, the fiscal criteria of the Delors Plan is difficult to justify on conventional Keynesian grounds unless there is a corresponding fiscal regime on a supranational level. In order to qualify for the final phase of monetary union, each country has been impelled to adhere to highly restrictive macroeconomic policy regimes. There has inevitably developed a powerful deflationary tendency within the Community which has culminated in the process of "competitive disinflation" as each country attempts to pursue a strategy to improve their export competitiveness through lower inflation in relation to their competitors (Fitoussi, 1993).

In order to escape from this straight-jacket of competitive disinflation, the co-ordination of national fiscal policies is essential. This would imply the recycling of surpluses from the structural core regions to the peripheral deficit regions. Since the EC budget cannot perform this redistributive function adequately, the whole process of economic integration hinges critically on the ability and willingness of national governments to co-ordinate and synchronise their respective fiscal policies. As long as asymmetries continue to exist, the stabilisation function of national fiscal policy will be necessary to counter country-specific disturbances and exogenous supply shocks.

Despite the imposition of quite harsh monetary and fiscal policies, all of the fifteen member countries, with the exception of Greece, have qualified for membership of the final phase of EMU. The performance of Italy has been quite impressive. From a budget deficit of 10 per cent in 1993, Italy has reduced the ratio to 2.5 per cent when the European Summit met in London in early May to finalise membership of the euro. In Italy, this fiscal target was accomplished through a severe curtailment of government expenditure and the imposition of a one-off "Eurotax" which raised about $3 billion. On the eve of the single currency, both Belgium and Italy with 118.1 per cent and Greece with 107.7 per cent have failed to meet their respective public debt/GDP ratios of 60 per cent, while for the budget deficit criteria, all of the 15 countries have achieved the target of 3 per cent of GDP.[5] Indeed, progress on budget deficits has been quite exceptional; the overall EU budget deficit fell from 6.1 per cent of GDP in 1993 to 2.7 per cent in 1997. Table 9.1 summarises the performance of each country in relation to the fiscal criteria in March 1998.

Table 9.1 The Maastricht Criteria on Public Debt and Budget Deficits (March 1998)

Maastricht Criteria	Debt as a % of GDP (60%)	Budget Deficit as a % of GDP (3%)
Austria	64.7	2.3
Belgium	118.1	1.3
Britain	53.0	0.6
Denmark	59.5	-1.1
Finland	53.6	-0.3
France	58.1	2.9
Germany	61.2	2.5
Greece	107.7	2.2
Ireland	59.5	-1.1
Italy	118.1	2.5
Luxembourg	7.1	-1.0
Netherlands	70.0	1.6
Portugal	60.0	2.2
Spain	67.4	2.2
Sweden	74.1	-0.5

Source: European Commission, 1998.

If fiscal discipline cannot be sustained, economic and monetary union will either be postponed or could disintegrate altogether. For instance, if a Member State withdraws from the EMU and resorts to debt monetisation in order to finance its fiscal deficit, this action could provoke a "bandwagon" effect by other deficit countries. As a result, financial stress in one country could raise doubts about the degree of financial solidarity across the Community and affect the financial credibility of government bonds.

---

5   Belgium and Italy were able to convince the EU authorities that their primary debt ratios were falling at a sufficient rate in order to qualify for membership.

Similarly, an interest rate increase in one country could induce a cumulative rise in other countries and increase the average Community rate if this is not accommodated by the Eurofed. With the liberalisation of capital markets there tends to develop "spill-over" effects in the absence of a coherent regulatory framework on the supranational level. Table 9.2 summarises the Maastricht criteria on long-term interest rates and inflation in April 1998.

Quite apart from fiscal co-ordination, the Maastricht accord relies almost exclusively on the efficacy of the market to discipline profligate governments. Under the theoretical conditions of perfect capital mobility, a fiscal expansion tends to appreciate the exchange rate and erode that country's competitiveness. A capital outflow will induce a rise in short-term interest rates and hasten the imposition of more restrictive policies. Conversely, an expansionary monetary policy will lead to a nominal exchange rate depreciation, if one assumes perfect capital mobility. In this case, there would be a temporary improvement in export competitiveness but these nominal gains would be offset by an increase in the rate of inflation. Furthermore, a rise in the external deficit in the medium term could induce a rise in long-term interest rates and a capital outflow. In both cases, the net effect is that each country pursues a strategy of disinflation in order to attract a capital inflow. For the deficit countries, however, the prolongation of disinflationary policies could prove to be counter-productive. The imposition of high interest rates could aggravate the external debt through a cumulative increase in their debt servicing ratio. In the most indebted countries of Italy, Greece, Belgium, Portugal Ireland and Spain, interest payments on their public debt had accounted for over 10 per cent of their respective GDPs and represented more than 20 per cent of their respective government expenditure in 1991 (Emerson, 1992, p.123).

Table 9.2   The Maastricht Targets for Inflation and Interest Rates; April 1998

Maastricht Criteria	Inflation* (%) Target (3.2%)		Long -term Interest Rates# Target (7.7%)
	1997	1998	1998
Austria	1.1	1.5	5.6
Belgium	1.4	1.3	5.7
Britain	1.8	2.3	7.0
Denmark	1.9	2.1	6.2
Finland	1.3	2.0	5.9
France	1.2	1.0	5.5
Germany	1.4	1.7	5.6
Greece	5.2	4.5	9.8
Ireland	1.2	3.3	6.2
Italy	1.8	2.1	6.7
Luxembourg	1.4	1.6	5.6
Netherlands	1.8	2.3	5.5
Portugal	1.8	2.2	6.2
Spain	1.8	2.2	6.3
Sweden	1.9	1.5	6.5

* Within 1.5% average of the lowest three.
# Within 2% average of inflation's lowest three.

Source: European Commission, 1988.

Despite these considerable obstacles, the European Summit in early May 1998 endorsed 11 of the 15 Member States to join the final stage of EMU which will involve the creation of the ECB and the issuing of the euro. Britain and Denmark will temporarily postpone their membership until they hold national referendums. Greece is expected to join in 2001 if it can qualify under the Maastricht criteria. In its fifth year of sustained economic growth, Britain's economic cycle is out of kilter with the rest of Europe with short-term interest rates at around 7 per cent and an appreciating exchange rate. The official launch of the euro will be on schedule in January 1, 1999. After that date, there will be a 3 year transition period during which national currencies will continue to exist as a subdivision of the euro. By January 1,

2002 Euro rates and coins will be issued and by July 1 of the same year, all national currencies will cease to have legal tender status.

III. Fiscal Federalism?

With the curtailment of fiscal policies and the eventual abolition of exchange rate policies on the national level, a corresponding regulatory regime is required for the Community as a whole. The other alternative would involve closer macroeconomic co-ordination between Member States. In the latter case it is difficult to envisage the willingness of surplus countries to finance the deficit countries. Asymmetries will continue to exist. Fiscal federalism would appear to be the logical corollary of monetary union. The Community budget would perform the redistributive and stabilisation functions now performed by national governments. This necessarily implies a form of political federation and an expansion in the legislative and budgetary powers of the European parliament. In such a schema, the EU budget would acquire a pivotal role. Quite apart from the enormous political obstacles involved over national sovereignty with the sensitive issue of fiscal federalism, the existing EU budget is simply inadequate to perform this strategic role.

Expenditure by the EU can be identified in two main categories: (1) the compulsory spending associated with the EAGGF guarantee section and (2) the non-compulsory expenditure in structural, social and regional policies. This division over expenditure reflects the political divide between the executive and legislative spheres of the EU. While the Council of Ministers determines the level of compulsory expenditure, the European Parliament has increased its legislative powers over non-compulsory expenditure. In 1990, the Community budget was estimated at 46.7b ECUs or about 1.2 per cent of the Community GDP and only 3.3 per cent of the combined total of the national budgets (Nugent, 1991, p.314). During the 1970s it became evident that the original system of "own" resources was insufficient to meet expenditure commitments. With the onset of recurrent recessions and economic stagnation, VAT revenue declined as private consumption was curtailed. At the same time, customs duties and agricultural levies also declined as agricultural protection was wind back in the wake of successive GATT Agreements. The budgetary crisis of the 1970s culminated in a new financial arrangement ratified at the Fontainbleau Summit of the European Council in June 1984. A key element of these reforms was an increase in the VAT ceiling to 1.4 per cent. The expansion of "own" resources was, however, insufficient to resolve the budgetary crisis.

A more comprehensive solution emerged with the implementation of the SEA and the Delors package in 1988 which proposed a source of revenue in the form of a variable "topping up" resource based on national contributions calculated as a proportion of their respective GDPs. The Delors package also sought to limit the expansion of agricultural spending to 74 per cent of the rate of growth of EU output, while doubling expenditure on the structural funds over a five year period (Artis & Lee, 1994, pp.376-77). This reflected a shift in the balance of power in favour of the European Parliament with an increase in the appropriation of non-compulsory revenue.

Despite these reforms, the EU budget is still inadequate to perform both a redistributive and stabilisation role for the Community as a whole. Given the size and structure of the Community budget, the automatic transfers required to act as "shock absorbers" to cushion the effects of asymmetrical regional shocks in the event of monetary union is quite negligible (Giovannini & Spaventa, p.101). According to the MacDougall Report of 1977, the EU budget would need to increase to at least 5 per cent of the Community GDP in order to perform this stabilising role (Artis & Lee, 1994, pp.384-85).

Conclusion

Competitive disinflation or "beggar-thy-neighbour" deflation has, over the past decade, become a substitute for competitive devaluations as member countries pursue a strategy to improve their export competitiveness in terms of lower inflation. Whereas competitive devaluations generate inflationary tendencies, competitive disinflation functions in the opposite direction by producing a cumulative process of deflation (Fitoussi, 1993). The discipline imposed by the ERM in which Germany acts as the nominal exchange rate anchor has imparted powerful deflationary impulses throughout the EMS zone. A more symmetrical regime with the pooling of national reserves and the creation of a single currency might ease these deflationary forces.

Competitive disinflation is deceptively simple. One country's exports represent another country's imports. This means that cumulative deflation caused by each country's pursuit of lower inflation in order to accumulate a trade surplus will, *ceteris paribus,* curtail imports by dampening the level of effective demand. This process of cumulative disinflation has contributed to the stagnation of the European economy in the 1990s. The broad outlines of this slump syndrome are evident by the severe curtailment of effective demand and the fall in the volume of intra-EU trade. At the same time, the failure to adhere to this monetarist-inspired hysteresis has provoked speculative forces which threaten to degenerate into monetary disintegration as the events of 1992-93 have already starkly illustrated.

The ultimate economic consequences of competitive disinflation are rising unemployment and a decline in productive investment. As tax revenues shrink as a result of the slump, each government is confronted by a fiscal crisis. Since the ability to resort to foreign borrowing has been constrained by the Maastricht Treaty and by the penalties imposed by a deregulated financial market, there has been an overwhelming trend toward public sector expenditure cut-backs and the privatisation of public assets in order to balance the national budget. Taken as a whole, these policies amount to a radical dismantling of the post-war system of the "social market" and the winding back of traditional Keynesian counter-cyclical policies.

From the standpoint of public policy, the central dilemma posed by monetary union is the problem of country-specific and asymmetrical shocks. In short, how will governments cope with business cycle stabilisation if the scope for fiscal policy is limited by the exchange rate constraint? After monetary union it will no longer be possible for national governments to pursue counter-cyclical policies. As already noted, the absence of independent monetary and exchange rate policy instruments will make it impossible to monetise public debts since the national debt will now be denominated in the euro. Even though endogenous, country-specific shocks will continue to occur after monetary union, national governments will be obliged to surrender a considerable degree of autonomy in their ability to pursue macroeconomic objectives. If fiscal co-ordination proves to be inadequate, then the other means by which to enact stabilisation policies is through a Community budget. This necessarily implies fiscal federalism. Unfortunately, the Community budget lacks the critical mass to perform this crucial role.

With the successful launch of the euro in January 1999, international portfolio investors will shift a substantial share of their holdings out of the dollar and into euros. At the same time, national governments in Europe will gradually sell "excess" reserves denominated in US dollars. Similarly, other central banks in the world will also shift their reserves away from dollar denominated assets and into euros. The real danger therefore lies in the emergence of excessive dollars circulating the financial markets which would have the effect of increasing international liquidity. As the demand for US dollars declines, the euro will tend to appreciate against the US dollar. According to Bergsten, an estimated net flow from dollars to Euros of around $500b to $1 trillion is likely to occur over the first two years after the launch of the single currency (Bergsten, 1997). Increased demand for the euro as a reserve currency will make it more expensive for the US to pay for large trade deficits. The euro is also likely to appreciate against the dollar because the EU countries are running a combined current account surplus of about 2 per cent of GDP in 1998.

The current, combined EU government bond market is estimated at $2 trillion which is slightly less than the US market but foreign exchange reserves are expected to dwarf those in the US. The non-government bond market, on the other hand, is expected to grow by about 14 per cent a year between 1998 and 2003, or from $US2.9 trillion to $5.6 trillion as a result of the conversion to the single currency (Economist, 11/4/98). Much of the growth will come from the corporate bond market which includes borrowings by banks and financial institutions, as well as industrial corporations. The euro will eventually challenge the dominance of the US dollar in international financial markets. In 1994, the US dollar accounted for about 57 per cent of total official holdings of foreign exchange of the IMF member countries, compared with 15 per cent for the German mark and 8 per cent for the yen. In terms of international means of payment, the dollar was used in 41 per cent of foreign exchange transactions, compared with about 18 per cent for the mark and 12 per cent for the yen. Even without Britain, the euro bloc will have a larger population, an equivalent GDP and a bigger share of world trade than the US. With the birth of the Euro, a tripolar system of international economic blocs will emerge with the US and Japan/East Asia constituting the other two poles.

Appendix A

Major Features of the Three EMU Stages

Economic	Monetary

Stage 1

• Completion of the internal market. • Strengthened competition policy. • Full implementation of the reform of the structural funds. • Enhanced co-ordination and surveillance. • Budgetary adjustment in the high debt/deficit countries.	• Capital market liberalisation. • Enhanced monetary and exchange rate co-ordination. • Re-alignments possible but infrequent. • All EC countries in the narrow band ERM. • Extended use of the ECU.

Stage 2

• Evolution and adoption of stage 1 policies. • Review of macroeconomic adjustments.	• Establishment of the Eurofed. • Possible narrowing of EMS bands.

Stage 3

• Definitive budgetary co-ordination system. • Possible strengthening of structural and regional policies.	• Eurofed in charge of monetary policy. • Irrevocably fixed exchange rates. • Introduction of the Euro.

Source: Emerson, 1992, p.40.

10 Uneven Development

Introduction

The centrifugal forces generated by the neo-liberal strategy will tend to sharpen regional disparities. Uneven development has emerged as one of the more critical dimensions of the Internal Market Programme, especially in the wake of the second enlargement with the membership of Portugal, Spain and Greece. The possible entry of several of the East European countries in the near future could further exasperate these regional disparities. At the same time, the dynamic of globalisation has increased competition and set in motion the purgative forces of "creative destruction." European industry will encounter quite intense global competition, most notably in the more labour intensive industries from the Newly Industrialised Countries of East Asia and elsewhere. With the liberalisation of capital markets and the launching of the euro, regions and countries which exhibit chronic balance of payments deficits could be transformed into regional problems. The Internal Market Programme therefore poses considerable economic consequences for the less developed regions and for those regions in the throes of industrial decline.

I. The Theory of Uneven Development

Uneven development has been an inherent feature of capitalist accumulation. The spatial dimension of economic development has been characterised by a core/periphery configuration. One of the seminal theories of this process was developed by G. Myrdal who argued that capital movements tend to increase regional inequality by concentrating in the more developed regions (Myrdal, 1957). These are identified as the centrifugal, "spread effects" caused by economic expansion in the core regions which diffuse technology, capital investment and a modern infrastructure to the outlying, less developed hinterlands: "In the centres of expansion, increased demand will spur investment, which in turn will increase incomes and demand and cause a second round of investment and so on. Saving will

161

increase as a result of higher incomes but will tend to lag behind investment in the sense that the supply of capital will steadily meet the brisk demand for it" (Ibid, p.28). However, the opposite logic of cumulative causation is evident in the less developed regions. These are identified as the "backwash effects" which merely reinforce the structural and socio-economic disadvantages of these regions.

Capital will tend to migrate from the less profitable to the more profitable sectors and regions of a spatially defined economy. According to Emmanuel, if labour remains relatively immobile, wages in the more technically advanced sectors of the economy will be generally higher than those in the less developed regions: "Since equivalence in capitalist production relations signifies not the exchange of equal quantities of labour, but that of equal aggregates of factors (labour and the use of capital), non-equivalence (unequal exchange) can only signify the exchange of unequal aggregates of the same factors" (Emmanuel, 1972, p.325). Uneven development can thus be defined as a sectoral disparity between different branches of production which exhibit differing capital/labour ratios. A dualism has evolved between the high wage, high productivity regions/countries, on the one hand, and the low wage, low productivity regions/countries, on the other hand. One of the most important agents of uneven development is the multinational corporation. As the modern bearer of the process of economic concentration and centralisation, the MNC is a powerful agency through which uneven development is fostered.

> Through its propensity to nestle everywhere, settle everywhere and establish connections everywhere, the multinational corporation destroys the possibility of national seclusion and self-sufficiency and creates a universal interdependence. But the multinational corporation is still a private institution with a partial outlook and represents only an imperfect solution to the problem of international co-operation. It creates hierarchy rather than equality and spreads its benefits unequally (Hymer, 1975, p.60).

Despite the increased propensity toward the globalisation of production, MNCs still require the traditional state functions to defend and legitimise property rights and provide a coherent regulatory framework. In other words, MNCs not only demand the dismantling of national barriers to the free movement of capital and technology, but also the conditions of social and political stability. However, the neo-liberal strategies favoured by MNCs inevitably erode national sovereignty and impose external constraints on the ability of national governments to pursue economic policies which promote employment and social cohesion. A powerful trade-off has therefore developed between the imperatives of national macroeconomic stability, on the one hand, and the maintenance of an external balance, on the other hand. As has been argued in the previous chapter, this exchange rate constraint has eroded traditional Keynesian counter-cyclical policies.

The liberalisation of trade and investment has fostered the emergence of a new international division of labour in which production in each country or region has become more specialised. This new hierarchy is beginning to emerge as MNCs restructure and rationalise their operations in order to take advantage of greater economies of scale across national borders. An organisational logic is also at work involving a high degree of centralisation in the decision-making process. There is a growing tendency to concentrate their key operational bases and research and development facilities in the more advanced economic regions and relegate their less skilled, assembly operations in the less developed regions. Uneven development is thus not only the natural consequence of capitalist accumulation, but also acquires an internal corporate dynamic of integration which implies a highly centralised structure of control and organisation (Vaitsos, 1980, p.36).

II. The Globalisation of European Capitalism

With the emergence of a frontierless Europe, the process of uneven development will be accentuated. MNCs are expected to increase their degree of vertical integration while the process of horizontal integration will diminish (Buckley, 1987, p.106). In other words, MNCs will tend to increase their economies of scale by concentrating on their core operations and restructuring their branch operations in order to improve their internal division of labour and take advantage of the larger internal European market. The reduction of location costs will result in greater specialisation and rationalisation between different branches of production. In the absence of locational advantages and government inducements, MNCs will no longer consider it to be profitable to invest in the more remote, less developed regions.

As national barriers are abolished, capital will become more mobile. Footloose investment will intensify competition between different regions to attract new investment. It would be reasonable to contend that in this atmosphere of increased competition and rationalisation, the core regions will benefit at the expense of the less favoured regions. The latter will compete against each other to attract the lower skilled, assembly operations by offering relatively cheaper wages. Spain and Portugal have already emerged as the preferred locations for these labour intensive production bases, while the newly emergent capitalist countries of Eastern Europe are beginning to offer similar investment opportunities. The automobile industry, for instance, has already assimilated the Eastern European countries into their global strategies of improved economies of scale and a more efficient intra-firm division of labour. The increased presence and penetration of Japanese industrial transplants in Europe over the past decade has impelled European volume producers to improve their regional division of labour. Eastern Europe offers both a large, inexpensive and skilled labour force as well as close proximity to the markets of the EU (Humbert, 1993, p.30).

The general trend toward greater concentration of capital during the merger boom of the 1980s has accelerated quite rapidly. According to Tsoukalis, the total number of mergers between the largest 1,000 firms in the EC increased from 115 in 1982 to 622 in 1990 (Tsoukalis, 1993, p.103). By 1990, the share of intra-EC mergers had exceeded those taking place within national borders. Indeed, intra-EC mergers were nearly twice as numerous as those involving non-EC partners (Cecchini, 1988, p.87). A study by INSEAD on 954 collaborative ventures between French, Italian, German and British firms in the period 1975 to 1986, revealed that more than 50 per cent were intra-EC, about 25 per cent were between EC firms and their US partners and 12.5 per cent were between EC firms and their Japanese counterparts (Dunning & Robson, 1988, p.87). The evidence appears to suggest that the SEA has provided a profound catalyst for the increased rate of concentration of capital. The other major catalyst has been the intensification of the competitive forces generated by non-European MNCs and the growing perception within Europe that industry has fallen behind in the more dynamic high technology sectors.

The emergence of Japanese MNCs in the late 1970s had intensified global oligopolistic competition and rivalry. In circumstances similar to the US investment boom of the 1960s, the Japanese challenge made international cross-investment an overriding imperative for the survival of European MNCs. The fate of "national champions" became increasingly dependent on their capacity to adapt to the forces of international competition. It was in this context that European consortiums and technological collaboration were fostered by the European Commission.

In the early 1980s, this growing technological gap with both the US and Japan in the high technology sectors had caused growing alarm in Europe. The EC trade deficit in information technology (IT) had increased from an estimated $4.1b in 1980 to about $7b in 1985. In 1985, the European share of the international semi-conductor market was only 9 per cent compared with the US share of 56 per cent and Japan at 33 per cent (Dunning & Robson, 1988, p.134). The Commission identified the smaller European national markets as an obstacle to the growth of individual firms which were, on average, much smaller and limited in their technological capacity. Furthermore, as the industrial life cycle of IT technologies was progressively shortened because of the innovative dynamics involved, the technological gap was expected to widen. Given the enormous amount of financial resources required to fund R & D expenditure, the Commissioner of Industry, Etienne Davignon, initiated the European Strategic Programme for Research in Information Technology (ESPRIT) in 1981 which sought to promote closer collaboration between twelve of Europe's largest IT firms.

Inspired by Japan's highly successful strategic trade policies which were guided by the Ministry of International Trade and Industry (MITI), the EC sought to emulate these policies. The Commission also promoted the development of European technical norms and standards in the IT sector which would furnish industry with the basic technical infrastructure required to bolster its international competitiveness. ESPRIT would augment the overall industrial strategy of the SEA. Phase One of this long-term strategic plan was expected to cover a ten year period (1984-93) in which more than $1.5b in funds was provided by the Commission. By 1987, however, these funds had been exhausted and a further $1.6b was injected into the project. Despite these large financial contributions, the ESPRIT project and other related high technology initiatives (ie, EUREKA, RACE, etc) have only had a marginal impact on the EU's international competitiveness. Unlike MITI, the relationship between big business and the Commission has been neither as close, nor as strategic.

In the semi-conductor industry, European firms continued to languish behind their rivals in the US and Japan. As US-Japanese trade rivalries intensified during the 1980s, European firms faced the prospect of not only being marginalised in the high technology sectors, but denied access to the US and Japanese markets. These fears were reinforced by the US-Japanese Semi-Conductor Agreement (SCA) signed in 1986 which imposed a reciprocal 20 per cent market share limit to foreign penetration of their respective markets. The SCA was an explicit violation of the GATT Agreements and represented a growing trend towards managed trade and bilateralism. It was in this environment of escalating US-Japanese trade rivalries and rising protectionism in the high technology sectors, that hastened the Commission to develop their own strategic trade policies.

Despite these policies, the EC's propensity to import high technology products has continued to increase. This has been accompanied by an unfavourable structural effect in which EC exports have increased in the more traditional, low demand manufacturing sectors. The EC experienced a 2.3 per cent decline in the market share of high technology exports between 1973 and 1984. Over the same period, the EC market share in the export of more traditional manufacturing products and in agriculture had increased by 3.9 per cent (Buigues & Goybet, 1989, p.243).

The EC's trade imbalance with Japan has emerged as a contentious issue for the EC authorities. While Japan accounted for 14.5 per cent of the Community's manufactured imports in 1986, only 3.2 per cent of EC manufactured imports had penetrated the Japanese market. The trade deficit with Japan increased from about 6b ECUs in 1979 to 9b in 1980 and 16b in 1984 (Richardson, 1989, p.6). In 1989 the trade deficit with Japan was estimated at around $25 billion (Camiller, 1989, p.13). Although Japanese investment in the EC is still quite small, the penetration of the European market in the high technology and automobile sectors has sent shock waves through European industry. Between 1980 and 1987, Japan's exports of manufactures to Europe more than doubled with quite spectacular increases in office and telecommunications (280%), cars (150%) and electronics (80%) (Winters & Venables, 1991, p.207).

Needless to say, the Japanese challenge has generated considerable friction within Europe which was reflected in the official release of the EC's external policy of the SEA in October 1988. The principle of trade reciprocity has informed EC trade policies which is defined as "non-discriminatory opportunities" for European firms to operate in foreign markets on the same basis as firms from those countries (Curzon-Price, 1988, p.41). By contrast, trade relations with the US have been more favourable. The stock of European investment in US manufacturing had increased three-fold between 1962 and 1985. Indeed, by 1985 the stock of European direct investment in US manufacturing was marginally higher than US direct investment in Europe (Dunning, 1988, p. 90). Most of this improvement occurred from the late 1970s onward as the decline of the US dollar encouraged European firms to establish industrial transplants in the American market.

The single market in Europe can be interpreted as a response and a possible catalyst to the formation of international trading blocs. A tripolar world system has evolved since the mid-1970s in which world production has been increasingly concentrated in the three main regional poles of North America, Japan/East Asia and Western Europe. Each geographically distinct core region is surrounded by a peripheral hinterland. Trade and investment appear to conform with a definite clustering pattern in which a core region is augmented by peripheral satellites. For instance, a core/periphery configuration is evident in relations between the EU and Eastern Europe, the US and Latin America and between Japan and East Asia. These regional constellations could coalesce into separate and competing trading blocs. Regionalism and multilateralism, however, are not mutually incompatible. Regional trading blocs might not imply autarchic policies but could, in fact, promote international trade liberalisation. On the other hand, the potential does exist for the emergence of exclusive trade blocs behind protectionist barriers.

III. The Regional Dimension

Within Europe, uneven development has historically manifested itself in a hierarchical pattern organised along three distinct social formations. First, there have evolved the underdeveloped regions which realise less surplus value than they produce and have provided a source of surplus labour for the industrialised core regions. Second, one can identify the semi-peripheral regions which maintain an unstable balance between the production, realisation and the transfer of surplus value to the core regions. At the very apex of this hierarchy reside the highly developed and technologically advanced core regions. These highly industrialised centres produce and realise their own surplus value as well as transfer and appropriate surplus value from the peripheral and semi-peripheral regions. A.G. Frank's thesis is quite valid when he states: "Thus at each point, the international, national and local capitalist system generates economic development for the few and underdevelopment for the many" (Frank, 1967, p.8).

In the official EC literature on regional policy, these three social formations more or less correspond with the backward agricultural regions, the declining and depressed industrial sectors and the technologically advanced, capital intensive metropolitan centres (Padoa-Schioppa, 1987). The poorer, less developed regions are located in Southern Italy, most of Greece, Portugal, Ireland and Spain (excluding the industrial eastern provinces) where average income is less than 70 per cent of the Community average. These regions represent about 20 per cent of the EU population or about 62 million inhabitants. With the accession of Spain, Portugal and Greece in the 1980s, the Community GDP has increased by 10 per cent but population has risen by 22 per cent and employment in agriculture by 57 per cent (Ibid, p.162).

Given the low levels of income and employment in these less developed regions, their potential as markets is quite limited. Since the propensity to save is relatively low, local investment will tend to remain low, thus reinforcing the vicious circle of poverty. As the chill winds of competition induced by market liberalisation threaten existing enterprises and incomes, the "backwash" effects will be reinforced. Locational disadvantages will deter investment as large firms take advantage of the single European market by improving their vertical integration and concentrating their core activities in the more lucrative markets. The more distant a market, the less likely it will be to attract private investment, while the absence of a modern infrastructure in these regions will only accentuate existing competitive and locational disadvantages.

The declining industrial regions are more difficult to categorise or identify. In general, these regions can be associated with the more mature industrial sectors in the steel, shipbuilding and textile industries. The official criteria for identifying these regions is by classifying them in the 70 to 100 per cent range of income per head of the Community average or by identifying the above average unemployment rates. According to this criteria, more than 10 per cent of the Community population live in these depressed regions which are located in the north and west of the UK, in the north of Spain, eastern Belgium, and in the north and east of France. Although in a state of decline and undergoing profound structural change, these industrial regions continue to augment and provide essential inputs to the more efficient, higher value-added and capital intensive manufacturing sectors. The steel industry, for instance, still provides backward linkages to the engineering and capital goods sectors.

It is also possible to distinguish another type of industrial enclave which is essentially dominated by foreign owned subsidiaries of MNCs and is usually surrounded by a cluster of smaller, local enterprises which service these foreign subsidiaries (Papadantonokis, 1985). A deficiency of local saving to generate endogenous investment has induced a type of "dependent industrialisation" characterised by a dual industrial structure which is highly dependent on government support. Despite undergoing industrialisation, there is a large outflow of labour from these regions. The declining industrial enclaves of Lisbon, Athens, Rome, Naples and Madrid tend to exhibit these dualistic features in which over-populated urban centres are encircled by the more backward rural hinterlands. In the event of market liberalisation, these regions appear to be the most vulnerable.

Uneven development has emerged as one of the most critical issues for the EU authorities. Historically, industrial concentration has developed within a triangular region between Paris, Frankfurt and Milan. The original Rome treaties recognised this regional dimension, most notably in the Italian *Mezzogiorno* and established the European Investment Bank (EIB) to promote economic development in these regions. The Agricultural Guidance section of the EAGGF was also created to foster agricultural restructuring and the development of infrastructure. These earlier programmes, however, were merely the outcome of specific national compromises and competing national claims. After the first enlargement in the 1970s, the whole issue of regional development was given greater focus with the creation of the European Regional Development Fund (ERDF). The total amount of resources devoted to regional and redistributive policies, however, remained quite negligible compared with the expenditure assigned to these programmes by national governments. In 1988 ERDF assistance amounted to only 0.09 per cent of the Community GDP or about 0.46 per cent of the EC fixed gross capital formation (Tsoukalis, 1993, p.212).

A new strategy on regional policy was launched as a central plank of the Internal Market Programme in 1985. This strategy coincided with the second enlargement of the Iberian peninsular and Greece. Its main contribution was the implementation of the Integrated Mediterranean Programmes (IMPs) which involved a further injection of $6.6b ECUs into existing development projects and loans. In February 1988 the Council of Ministers approved a doubling of the resources to the three major regional funds. EC expenditure on these structural funds accounted for about 27 per cent of the EC budget, as Table 10.1 illustrates. The political significance of these reforms was that it liberated regional policy from its former propensity to be the object of competing national claims. The abolition of national quotas could provide the basis for a more cohesive regional policy. Regional disparities, however, are likely to become more acute as a direct consequence of the neo-liberal strategy adopted by the Internal Market Programme.

Table 10.1 The Community Budget (1993)

Area of Spending	ECU (millions)	Percentage
EAGGF (Agricultural Fund)	34,660	53.2
Structural Operations	17,965	27.6
Policies with Multiannual Allocations	2,700	4.0
Other Policies	2,048	7.7
Repayments and Administration	3,833	5.9

Source: Britton & Mayes, 1993, pp.76-77.

The impact of monetary union on these less developed regions could be quite adverse. If labour remains relatively immobile but capital becomes highly mobile, then wages will tend to diverge between different regions. Capital will migrate to the more profitable regions, attracted by the high levels of demand and the close proximity to expanding markets. In the absence of national exchange rate policy instruments to adjust to an adverse terms of trade, monetary union will transform balance of payments crises into regional problems. The less favoured regions/countries will become more vulnerable to cost-push inflation caused by a shift in demand to the more prosperous regions/countries. As national regimes of regulation and government intervention are gradually abolished, the competitiveness of these regions will doubtless suffer.

At the same time, the recycling of surpluses from the metropolitan core regions to the less developed hinterlands through the Community budget will not be sufficient to offset the adverse structural impact caused by monetary union. Quite simply, the redistributive powers and the limited fiscal resources of the EC budget cannot perform this role on the required scale and scope. Despite the reform of the structural funds, it is highly unlikely that these redistributive mechanisms will be enough to stabilise, let alone reverse the process of uneven development. Although some of the less developed regions might in fact benefit from the creation of production bases attracted by lower real wages and lower costs of production, the vast majority of these regions will be condemned to a perennial state of economic stagnation. In other words, the "backwash" effects will continue to prevail over the "spill-over" effects.

Conclusion

From a historical standpoint, uneven development has been an inherent feature of capitalist accumulation. In the past, national governments have pursued policies which sought to promote a more balanced development through quite complex and extensive methods of State intervention. Indeed, the creation of a domestic market through a strategy of import substitution and national regimes of regulation and protectionism, had informed the countries which now constitute the core regions. It is quite plausible to contend that industrialisation would not have been possible in the absence of these forms of State intervention (Senghaas, 1985). The abolition of these forms of regulation could prevent the adoption of similar strategies of import substitution and the evolution of a domestic market by the less developed countries of the EU. These countries and regions could be condemned to a peripheral and semi-peripheral status if either strategies of export-led growth based on the inflow of foreign capital fail to promote development, or if structural and regional policies on the Community level prove to be ineffectual. In this chapter it has been argued that, with few exceptions, it is difficult to envisage an optimistic scenario of rapid economic growth emanating from these depressed regions as long as the neo-liberal paradigm of "negative integration" continues to inform the architects of the single market.

The globalisation of European capitalism will intensify competitive forces and hasten a phase of rationalisation and concentration of economic power. It is precisely this dialectic between globalisation, on the one hand, and regionalism, on the other hand, that constitutes the rationalising dynamic of the European single market. In order to restore and improve their international competitiveness, European MNCs are compelled to rationalise production and improve their economies of scale. A single, unified European market ostensibly offers considerable scope to achieve this process of industrial restructuring and technological upgrading. Yet at the same time, the purgative forces generated by this neo-liberal strategy will merely accentuate the process of uneven development. As the rate of concentration and centralisation of capital gains momentum, whole industries and regions might no longer be competitive in the European market, let alone in global markets. The whole vortex of uneven development therefore asserts itself both from within and from without the internal market through the agency of the multinational corporation. It is quite possible that these centrifugal forces could threaten the prospects of economic and monetary union in Europe.

Conclusion

Quite contrary to prevailing neo-functionalist interpretations of the origins and evolution of the single market in Europe, this study has stressed the primacy of the nation state in post-war European history. Rather than an internal logic of integration, it has been argued that the process of integration has been primarily determined by the configuration of international economic and politico-military relations. Post-war economic reconstruction demanded a supranational response. This overriding necessity was dictated by two fundamental conditions. First, in order to avoid a relapse into the syndrome of economic nationalism and autarchy, the American architects of the European Recovery Programme (ERP) fostered closer inter-State economic co-operation (Lipgens, 1982). As a result, the pre-war problems of access to raw materials, investment outlets and markets could be resolved within a supranational framework. At the very core of this problem was the economic reconstruction of the West German economy and the political rehabilitation of the West German State (Bulmer & Paterson, 1987). Franco-German rapprochement was therefore essential.

The second condition in this post-war settlement involved the formation of an anti-Soviet bloc in Western Europe by the Americans in order to deter the perceived threat of Soviet expansionism. Closer European political and military co-operation became a necessary precondition in the formation of the Western alliance after the war. With the onset of Cold War rivalries, the Americans actively supported the anti-Communist forces in the ranks of the Christian Democratic and centrist alliances which emerged as the dominant political power blocs over the next two decades. The Christian Democratic ascendancy in Western Europe provided the political rationale in the birth of the Common Market. This was most evident in the creation of the Common Agricultural Policy (CAP) in which the powerful agricultural lobbies formed a strategic power base for the Christian Democratic parties.

Quite apart from the geo-political imperatives of the Cold War, the American authorities viewed the reconstruction of the European market as an essential means by which to resolve their own impending crisis of overproduction. The European market would provide an outlet for

173

American exports and resolve America's domestic problems of surplus capacity generated during the war (Kolko, 1972). Indeed, the trade imbalance between Europe and the United States only aggravated the dollar shortage in Europe which imposed severe constraints on their ability to launch a programme of economic reconstruction. It was in this context that the Marshall Plan was conceived as a means of resolving the burgeoning US trade surpluses by providing loans and reconstruction aid to European governments so that they could purchase American exports.

Customs union theory had informed the American architects of the recovery programme. It was assumed that a more unified European market would increase the propensity to import American goods while at the same time, improve the economies of scale beyond the limits imposed by the existing national markets within Europe. In other words, American economic planners sought to re-cast European capitalism in their own image through the construction of a "United States of Europe". The "politics of productivity" had governed the American strategy in Europe insofar as the trade imbalance and the dollar shortage were essentially designated as a European problem of production and productivity (Maier, 1987).

Although the American sponsored recovery programme failed to resolve the trade imbalance and the dollar shortage, the Americans had laid the foundations for a more liberal international economic architecture under the aegis of *Pax Americana*. This new order was enshrined by the institutions of the IMF/World Bank and the GATT Agreements, while the US dollar would perform the international role of reserve currency and a means of payments under the post-war Bretton Woods accords. It was in this liberal international environment which ultimately provided the necessary conditions for closer European economic and political integration. American mediation therefore provided the rationalising dynamic in the process of post-war European integration.

Within Western Europe, Franco-German rapprochement was the pivot around which supranational forms of organisation revolved. The formation of the ECSC provided the blueprint for further sectoral forms of integration. For the French authorities, the pooling of coal and steel resources rescued the Monnet Plan. Access to the coal and steel resources of the Saarland was essential for France's reconstruction plans. Moreover, international control over Germany's crucial war-making industries allayed French fears of the possible resurgence of German militarism. From the standpoint of the newly emergent West German State, the internationalisation of the Ruhr implied the dismantling of the allied occupation and access to the strategic coal and steel resources. Membership of the ECSC also conferred a considerable degree of legitimacy to the West German State. The rehabilitation of the West German economy provided the unifying logic to the post-war phase of European economic reconstruction and recovery. With the onset of the dollar shortage, the European economies switched to the importation of German capital goods which, in turn, re-equipped and modernised European industry. At the same time, Germany provided an expanding market for European exports. The phase of post-war economic recovery during the 1950s was thus set in motion through a dynamic process of trade interpenetration with Germany acting as the engine of growth for the European economies as a whole. Consequently, the pre-war problem of access to raw materials, investment outlets and markets was resolved on a supranational level. Supranationalism, however, did not imply the supersession of the existing system of nation-states. Indeed, it would be reasonable to contend that these supranational forms of mediation were a necessary means by which the primacy of the nation-state could be restored (Milward, 1992).

The liberalisation and rapid growth in intra-European trade can be readily identified as the *sine qua non* in the formation of the customs union. In terms of the classical formulation of customs union theory, the dynamic of trade creation had more than compensated for the adverse impact of trade diversion (Viner, 1950). Liberal economic doctrines had informed the strategy of "negative integration" which had been adopted by the architects of the Rome treaties (Holland, 1975). This strategy involved the progressive removal of quantitative restrictions to the circulation of capital, labour, goods and services within the Common Market and the creation of a Common External Tariff (CET). After the signing of the Rome Treaties in 1958, the Common Market emerged as the largest trading bloc in the world.

Much of the earlier evolution of the single market was overshadowed by de Gaulle's divergent vision of a confederated Europe constructed on the foundations of the nation-state (Pinder & Pryce, 1969). De Gaulle's intransigent opposition to federalist aspirations culminated in the famous Luxembourg Compromise of 1967 which established the national right of veto over Community legislation (Camps, 1967). As a result, progress toward closer political integration was postponed. It was not until after de Gaulle's resignation in 1969 that the issues of Community own resources, British accession to the Common Market and the increased legislative powers of the European parliament over the Community budget could be resolved. It can be surmised that Gaullism represented the political re-assertion of the European nation-state. In stark contrast to neo-functionalist interpretations, the Community evolved as a loose confederation of nation-states which was reflected in the very limited powers conferred onto the European parliament and the supreme executive powers vested in the Council of Ministers. Furthermore, the lack of political autonomy exhibited by the Commission tended to inhibit the process of political "spill-over" advocated by the proponents of the neo-functionalist strategy. In the final analysis, political integration failed to penetrate the sphere of "high politics" in terms of a common defense and foreign policy.

The emergence of trans-Atlantic trade rivalry signalled a decisive turning point in the evolution of the single market. Economic rivalry was triggered by the onset of the dollar crisis and the unprecedented inflow of US direct investment in the EEC during the 1960s. The American challenge evoked fears in Europe of the spectre of industrial colonisation and induced a wave of mergers and corporate take-overs in Europe in order to counter the US corporate invasion. At the same time, the demise of the post-war system of fixed exchange rates had provoked a series of exchange rate crises which threatened to undermine the Common Market. In response, European leaders sought to create a zone of monetary stability within Europe. As the international economic crisis intensified in the early 1970s, it became increasingly evident that the loss of national sovereignty over economic policies could be recovered on a supranational level (Mandel, 1970). The single market therefore evolved from a predominantly political bloc governed by the exigencies of the Cold War into an organised trading bloc.

Economic and monetary union represented the second stage in the neo-functionalist strategy in the completion of the single market. Monetary union would eventually prefigure political federalism. The first experiment in monetary union, however, was a failure. International exchange rate volatility continued unabated after the formal abandonment of the Bretton Woods system in 1973. It was now possible for the US monetary authorities to pursue a policy of "benign neglect" and allow the dollar to progressively depreciate. By doing so, the US economy could recover its loss of export competitiveness in international markets (Parboni, 1981). This policy merely induced an inflationary upsurge and generated further instability in international financial markets. The European authorities attempted to stabilise intra-Community exchange rates with the introduction of a fixed exchange rate regime - the "snake in the tunnel" - which was designed to limit the degree of intra-Community exchange rate divergence and foster a more coherent means of exchange rate concertation. EMU was essentially a Franco-German accord. While the French authorities sought to stabilise the CAP, the Germans were more concerned about the inflationary impact of speculative capital inflows. At the same time, successive exchange rate appreciations had undermined Germany's export competitiveness. For the German authorities, EMU was an important means by which to preserve their export competitiveness within Europe and sterilise capital inflows by making the German mark a closer substitute for other EEC currencies. The adverse impact of an exchange rate appreciation would be offset by a superior anti-inflationary performance.

The debates between "economists" and "monetarists" which had preceded the official implementation of the Werner Report had reflected the divergent strategies advocated by the French and German authorities toward EMU. Represented by the Dutch and German experts, the "economists" had advocated a gradualist strategy in which closer economic union would create the conditions for eventual monetary union. Their strategy implied a gradual convergence of economic policies between member countries with a strong anti-inflationary bias. The "monetarists", represented by French experts, on the other hand, had advocated the immediate realisation of monetary union with the irrevocable fixing of exchange rate parities between the member countries. At stake in these debates was the issue of which country would incur the greatest burden of structural adjustment in the event of monetary union. This division reflected the conflicting imperatives of the deficit and surplus countries.

According to the seminal theory of optimum currency areas, monetary union implies that the surplus countries should pursue a reflationary policy in order to ease the adverse structural impact of higher unemployment experienced in the deficit countries (Mundel, 1961). In order to prevent the emergence of asymmetries, the recycling of surpluses to the deficit countries is required, either in the form of providing additional credit or through an increase in the level of effective demand in the surplus countries. The ultimate solution to this problem of structural adjustment is identified by Mundel in terms of the increased mobility of labour. An asymmetrical shock will, *ceteris paribus,* induce a migration from the deficit to the surplus countries/regions. In the absence of a high degree of labour mobility and the unwillingness of the surplus countries/regions to increase their level of effective demand, these asymmetries will tend to become more acute under a fixed exchange rate regime or in the event of monetary union. Deprived of the ability to rely on an exchange rate devaluation in order to adjust to an adverse economic shock, the deficit countries/regions will experience a more painful process of adjustment in terms of higher unemployment.

Given these divergent national economic tendencies, the issue of monetary union remained unresolved. With the onset of recession and the oil price shocks, the "snake in the tunnel" could no longer promote exchange rate stability and eventually succumbed to speculative attacks. The first experiment in EMU ended in failure. Indeed, EMU had evolved into an exclusive DM-zone. After the failure of the first experiment, it was considered highly unlikely that another attempt would be made. However, the renewed instability of the US dollar had generated a new wave of speculation in 1978. The steep slide in the dollar had threatened German exports and induced another round of financial and exchange rate instability.

With the election of the Social Democratic government of Schmidt in Germany, the issue of EMU was resurrected despite powerful opposition from the Bundesbank. After the election of D'Estaing in France, Schmidt had found an accommodating ally in the revitalisation of the EMU project. This favourable political configuration established the conditions for the birth of the European Monetary System (EMS). As the international economic environment became more propitious after the cyclical recovery of 1982-83, intra-Community economic trends began to converge once again. Unlike its "snake" predecessor, the EMS was conferred with greater financial resources and had exhibited a higher degree of flexibility in intra-ERM exchange rates. The most innovative feature of the EMS was the introduction of the Exchange Rate Mechanism (ERM) which was a central system of bilateral exchange rates in which the degree of fluctuation was limited to within (+/-) 2.25 per cent. These bilateral rates were expressed in terms of the European Currency Unit (ECU) which was issued by the European Monetary Co-operation Fund (EMCF) to which the central banks deposited 20 per cent of their gold and dollar reserves.

Germany emerged as the dominant country in an asymmetrical regime in which the DM performed the role of nominal exchange rate anchor for the EMS as a whole. While the German authorities were able to adjust their exchange rate policies through interest rate adjustments, the deficit countries increasingly resorted to the imposition of exchange rate and capital controls. Similarly, while the German authorities pursued a trade-off between economic growth and lower inflation, the deficit countries were compelled to sacrifice economic growth to achieve exchange rate stability. At the same time, the Bundesbank was trenchantly opposed to the internationalisation of the German mark because of the inflationary risks involved. In contrast to the fixed exchange rate system under Bretton Woods in which the US economy provided an expansionary impetus for the international economy, Germany imparted a disinflationary impulse throughout the EMS zone. Although this process of "competitive disinflation" fostered a greater degree of exchange rate cohesion and discipline within the EMS with the convergence of national inflation rates, the ultimate costs were evident in terms of economic stagnation and rising unemployment, or what became known as the onset of "Eurosclerosis".

The inherent asymmetrical dynamics of the EMS could no longer be contained as a vicious circle developed between the trade deficits in Italy and France, on the one hand, and the trade surpluses in Germany and the Netherlands, on the other hand. In the absence of a reflationary policy in Germany, the deficit countries were forced to rely on capital controls to maintain their respective exchange rate parities. Indeed, the impact of this exchange rate constraint on the ability of a deficit country to enact an expansionary programme was quite graphically portrayed in the failure of the French Socialist policies of "Keynesianism in one country" during the early 1980s.

Germany therefore consolidated its hegemonic position in Europe in the 1980s by accumulating successive trade surpluses. This economic dominance was translated into the imposition of German ideological preferences in the form of quite severe disinflationary policies. In short, the EMS had evolved into an asymmetrical DM-zone which provided a sphere of exchange rate stability to which the majority of German exports were destined, while partially insulating the German economy from the destabilising impact of successive dollar devaluations after 1985. An analysis of the Maastricht blueprint for EMU reveals that the "convergence criteria" had institutionalised this German ideological paradigm.

It was the onset of the phenomena of "Eurosclerosis" from the mid-1970s onward that provided the catalyst for the Internal Market Programme in the mid-1980s. The relatively poor performance of the European capitalist economies in relation to their American and Japanese rivals had provoked considerable debate about the competitiveness and structural weaknesses of European industry. This lack of innovative and competitive dynamism would ostensibly be resolved with the implementation of a neo-liberal programme which involved the dismantling of national regimes of regulation and protectionism. With a general shift to the political right during the 1980s and a crisis afflicting the social democratic alternative, the neo-liberal programme gained the political ascendancy. Its proponents had advocated the liberalisation of the European market through the removal of existing non-tariff barriers, the opening-up of public procurement policies and the liberalisation of capital markets. This strategy also implied the winding back of the power of organised labour and the deregulation of labour markets.

According to the influential Cecchini Report (1988), these ostensible "efficiency" gains would be secured through greater rationalisation and economies of scale which would promote technological innovation and economic growth within a more uniform internal market enshrined by the 279 proposals that formed the basis of the Single European Act (SEA). The neo-liberal strategy doubtless corresponded with the objectives of powerful transnational corporations based in Europe which sought to increase their penetration of the European market and improve their competitiveness with foreign rivals. The existing national regimes of accumulation were no longer considered to be compatible with the imperatives of globalisation. It is doubtful, however, if these national regimes of regulation will be reproduced on a supranational level. In the absence of strategically powerful and coherent supranational state apparatuses, the European market will be quite vulnerable to the penetration of international capital and will tend to inhibit the competitiveness of European firms in the global market.

The critique of this neo-liberal strategy is informed by the fundamental dilemma of "territorial non-coincidence" (Murray, 1971). The crisis of European capitalism appears to involve a breakdown of existing national forms of mediation. This study has identified three critical dimensions to the efficacy of the neo-liberal strategy. First, is monetary union possible in the absence of a corresponding fiscal framework on a supranational level? Second, the issue of a European "social space" will manifest itself as national forms of labour market regulation and the whole plethora of wages, working conditions and social legislation will be subjected to the impersonal forces of the market. A European social space is therefore necessary in order to prevent the destructive phenomena of "social dumping". In this sense, the narrow imperatives of labour market deregulation and labour mobility which inform the neo-liberal strategy are quite simply inadequate in the social sphere. The third issue involves the regional consequences of this process of market liberalisation and monetary union. The evidence appears to suggest that these regional disparities will tend to widen.

The efficacy of the neo-liberal strategy ultimately confronts the limits of its own narrow economism. Quite contrary to the optimistic projections made by the proponents of Project 1992, this study contends that the liberal and deregulationist logic will merely accentuate regional disparities, erode established social legislation and norms, and severely limit the scope for traditional Keynesian policies of fiscal stabilisation and full employment. The restoration of the competitive dynamism of European capitalism through the neo-liberal strategy cannot be taken for granted. The process of negative integration will merely hasten the emergence of centrifugal forces which could threaten further progress toward European union. It is possible to construct three scenarios in the future evolution of the single market.

Scenario One: The Rise of Nationalism and the Disintegration of Supranationalism

In this scenario, the dormant though still powerful currents of nationalism and ethnic rivalries could gain the ascendancy. A relapse into the syndrome of nationalist/imperialist rivalry which had engulfed the continent in the inter-war years is quite possible. This scenario would presuppose an intensification of the current capitalist crisis and the collapse of the prevailing liberal-democratic forms of government. Although the objective conditions and the subjective forces for this kind of scenario appear quite remote, nationalist political tendencies have already emerged in the wake of the collapse of the Soviet bloc. In Germany, neo-fascism has reared its ugly head but is still only confined to the extreme political fringes. In France, the National Front has gained momentum and approached the very threshold of mainstream politics, while in Italy, the Italian Social Movement (MSI) has also acquired considerable political legitimacy.

The deep-seated structural crisis in Europe has resonated in the social and political spheres. With the relative demise of traditional social democratic policies and the ascendancy of the neo-liberal economic paradigm, the post-war consensus based on "social market" policies has been undermined. A single currency and a single market implies the supersession of national forms of State power and the creation of a supranational regime of governance. The neo-liberal strategy of negative integration, however, does not propose to substitute these national forms of capitalist regulation on a supranational level. The political crisis is therefore an expression of the contending national/supranational forms of State power. Although European statehood would not necessarily abolish the existing system of national politics, the remorseless logic of globalisation will tend to accentuate these social and regional disparities. Deprived of its traditional armour of sovereignty, nationalism could be re-activated to restore the primacy of the nation-state.

The growing ranks of the unemployed will doubtless provide a fertile breeding ground for the growth of these extremist nationalist forces. Scapegoats can be readily targeted with the presence of foreign workers. With the general shift to the political right, racism has become the dominant ideological expression of this resurgent nationalism. In this sense, the recent Balkan conflict represents the most extreme manifestation of this ethnic/nationalist revival. The triumph of these forces could hasten the Balkanisation of Europe. At present, the likelihood of this disturbing scenario appears quite remote. A major economic catastrophe or war could, however, unleash these forces into the maelstrom of history.

Scenario Two: A Confederalist Europe Based on German Hegemony

A more likely scenario which conforms with the argument developed in this study would involve a process of historical continuity with minor variations. The most significant development over the past two decades has been the emergence of German economic dominance. Although the Franco-German axis still constitutes the pivot around which the process of European integration revolves, the German economy occupies the very core of Europe. This is evident not only in the relative size of the German economy but also in the strategic role performed by German capital goods in the dynamics of capital accumulation on a European scale. A central argument of this study has been that the German economy has provided an engine of growth for Europe since the war. The Common Market represented a historical resolution to the issues of markets, investment outlets, and access to raw materials which had been the fundamental causes of inter-state rivalry before the war. In this crucial sense, the making of Europe was the answer to Germany's own making after the war.

German economic dominance is reflected in the politics of monetary union. The German mark has emerged as the nominal exchange rate anchor for the European monetary system while German ideological preferences have prevailed in the creation of a European central bank. Germany is at the very core of Europe surrounded by a concentric circle of peripheral and semi-peripheral countries. In this configuration, the northern industrial regions constitute the centre with the peripheral and semi-peripheral countries in the south and west gravitating around this epicentre. A third concentric circle would constitute the newly emergent capitalist economies of eastern Europe. Given this new enlarged European sphere, the likelihood of European federalism appears difficult to accomplish. A loose confederation is the most likely outcome with Germany acting as the hegemonic centre. A more accurate analogy might be made with the nineteenth century formation of the German Zollverein in which Prussia established a base for future expansion. The ultimate question is whether the

European Union will become a platform for future German economic expansion.

Scenario Three: European Federalism?

Despite the ideals and aspirations of European federalists, the likelihood of European statehood appears as remote as ever. Indeed, much of the ostensible progress toward European federalism has been imbued with mythology. In the past, European countries have pursued an imperialist policy of territorial acquisition and expansion in order to resolve their domestic problems of markets and access to raw materials. One of the central aims of the post-war political settlement was to reconcile these inter-imperialist rivalries within a pan-European framework. German militarism, in particular, could now be contained and to paraphrase Schuman, "make war not only unthinkable but materially impossible". To this end, supranationalism has succeeded in fostering peace and prosperity within Western Europe. Conceived in the destructive cataclysm engendered by modern war, the federalist cause attracted considerable popular support for a brief period but soon withered away as the nation-state re-asserted its pre-eminent role in European politics. In contrast to federalist interpretations, this study has generally supported Milward's contention that supranationalism represented a European rescue of the nation-state (Milward, 1992). The federalist cause might still evoke noble sentiments but has receded in the course of history.

Bibliography

Aglietta M. (1979), *A Theory of Capitalist Regulation*, New Left Books, London.

Al-Chalabi F.J. (1980), *OPEC and the International Oil Industry*, Oxford University Press, New York.

Aldcroft D.H. (1978), *The European Economy: 1914-70*, Croom Helm Ltd., London.

Ambrose S.E. (1971), *Rise to Globalism: American Foreign Policy; 1938-70*, Penguin, London.

Amin S., Arrighi G., Frank A.G. & Wallerstein I., ed., (1982), *Dynamics of Global Crisis*, Monthly Review Press, New York.

Arestis P. & Chick V., ed., (1995), *Finance, Development and Structural Change*, Edward Elgar, London.

Armstrong P., Glyn A. & Harrison J. (1991), *Capitalism Since 1945*, Basil Blackwell, USA.

Arndt H.W. (1963), *The Economic Lessons of the 1930s*, Royal Institute of International Affairs, Frank Cass, Ltd., London.

Arrighi G. (1978), *The Geometry of Imperialism*, New Left Books, London.

_____ ed, (1985), *Semiperipheral Development*, Sage Publishers, USA.

Artis M. & Lee N., ed., (1994), *The Economics of the European Union*, Oxford University Press, New York.

Atkinson A.B. & Brunetta R., ed., (1991), *Economics for the New Europe*, McMillan & Co., London.

Balassa B., "American Direct Investment in the Common Market", *Banca Nazionale Del Lavoro*, June, 1996.

_____ "Trade Creation and Trade Diversion in the European Community", *The Economic Journal*, Vol. 77, March, 1967.

Blanden-Hovell R., in Artis & Lee, ed., 1994.

Bank of England Quarterly Bulletin, "The Exchange Rate Mechanism in the European Monetary System", November, 1990.

Baran P.A. (1973), *The Political Economy of Growth*, Penguin, London.

Baran P.A., & Sweezy P. (1975), *Monopoly Capital*, Penguin, London.

Barratt-Brown M. (1970), *After Imperialism*, Redwood Press, London.

185

Berger S., ed., (1981), *Organising Interests in Western Europe*, Cambridge University Press, London.Bergsten C.F., *EMU and the International Monetary System*, IMF Symposium, March, 1997.

Block F. (1977), *Origins of Economic Disorder*, University of California Press, New York.

Boltho A., ed., (1982), *The European Economy*, Oxford University Press, New York.

_____ "Western Europe's Economic Stagnation", *New Left Review*, No. 201, 1993.

Bornstein S., Held D. & Krieger J., ed., (1984), *The State in Capitalist Europe*, Sage Publishers, London.

Britton A. & Mayes D. (1992), *Achieving Monetary Union in Europe*, Sage Publishers, London.

Brocker J. & Peschel K., in Molle & Cappellin, ed., 1985.

Bryant R.C. & Portes R., ed., (1987), *Global Macroeconomics: Policy Conflict & Co-operation*, MacMillan Press, Ltd., London.

Buckley P.J. & Artisien P. (1987), *North-South Direct Investment in the European Communities*, MacMilan Press, London.

Buiges T. & Goybet A., in Jacquemin & Sapir, ed., 1989.

Bukharin N., "World Economy and National Economy", in Radice, ed., 1975.

Bulmer P.J. & Paterson W. (1987), *The Federal Republic of Germany and the EC*, Allen & Unwin, London.

Business Week, "Why the Dollar Falls", July 23, 1973.

Camiller P., "Beyond 1992: The Left and Europe", *New Left Review*, No. 175, 1989.

Camps M. (1967), *European Unification in the Sixties*, Oxford University Press, London.

_____ (1965) *What Kind of Europe?* Royal Institute of International Affairs, London.

Canzoneri M.B. & Rogers C.A., "Is the European Community an Optimal Currency Area?", *American Economic Review*, No.80, June, 1990.

Carr E.H. (1951), *The Twenty Years Crisis: 1919 -39*, MacMillan & Co., London.

_____ (1981), *What is History?*, Penguin, London.

Cecchini P. (1988), *1992: The European Challenge*, Commission of the EC, Brussels.

Chevalier J.M., (1975), *The New Oil Stakes*, Allen Lane, London.

Cline W.R., ed., (1983), *Trade Policy in the 1980s*, Institute for International Affairs, USA.

Coffey P. (1977), *Europe and Money*, MacMillan, London.

_____ (1987), *The European Monetary System - Past, Present and Future*, Kluwer Academic Publishers, London.

Coffey P. & Presley J.R. (1971), *European Monetary Integration*, McMillan, London.

Committee for the Study of Economic and Monetary Union, *Report on Economic and Monetary Union in the EC*, (The Delors Report), European Commission, Brussels, 1989.

Curzon-Price V., *1992: Europe's Last Chance?*, Institute of Economic Affairs, Occasional Paper, No.81, 1988.

Daltrop A. (1992), *Politics and the European Community*, Longman Group, Ltd., Hong Kong.

De Cecco M., "Origins of the Post-War Payments System", *Cambridge Journal of Economics*, No.3, 1979.

De Cecco M. & Giovannini A., ed., (1989), *A European Central Bank?*, Cambridge University Press, London.

De Grauwe P. (1992), *The Economics of Monetary Integration*, Oxford University Press, London.

De Grauwe P. & Papademos L., ed., (1990), *The European Monetary System in the 1990s*, Longman Inc., New York.

de la Mahotiere S. (1968), *Towards One Europe*, Penguin, London.

Delzell C.F., "The European Federalist Movement in Italy: First Phase; 1918-47", *Journal of Modern History*, September, 1960.

Dermine J., ed., (1990), *European Banking in the 1990s*, Basil Blackwell, Oxford.

Deutsch K.W. (1969), *Political Community and the North Atlantic Area*, Greenwood Press, New York.

Diamandouros P.N., "The Southern European NICs", *International Organisation*, No.40, Spring, 1986.

Dornbusch R., in Giovazzi et al, 1988.

Dunning J.H. (1988), *Multinationals, Technology and Competitiveness*, Unwin Hyman, London.

Dunning J.H. & Robson P., ed., (1988), *Multinationals and the European Community*, Basil Blackwell, Oxford.

Edwards J. & Fischer K. (1994), *Banks, Finance and Investment in Germany*, Cambridge University Press, London.

EEC Commission (1972), *Report to the Council and Commission on the Realisation by Stages of Economic and Monetary Union in the Community*, (The Werner Report), Brussels.

Emerson M., ed., (1984), *Europe's Stagflation*, Clarendon Press, Oxford.
_____ ed., (1992), *One Market, One Money*, Oxford University Press, New York.
Emerson M. & Hume C. (1991), *The ECU Report*, Commission of the EC, Pan Books, London.
Emmanuel A., (1972), *Unequal Exchange: A Study of the Imperialism of Trade*, Monthly Review Press, New York.
Evans D., ed., (1973), *Britain in the EEC*, Victor Gollancz, Ltd., London.
Feldstein M., "EMU and International Conflict", *Foreign Affairs*, November/December, 1997.
Ferri P., ed., (1990), *Prospects for the European Monetary System*, St. Martin's Press, New York.
Fitoussi J.P., ed., (1993), *Competitive Disinflation*, Oxford University Press, New York.
Frank A.G., (1967), *Capitalism and Development in Latin America*, Monthly Review Press, New York.
Franko L.G. (1976), *The European Multinationals*, Harper & Row, London.
Frantzen D.J. (1990), *Growth and Crisis in Post-War Capitalism*, Dartmouth Press, UK.
Fratianni M., Von Hagen J. & Waller C., "The Maastricht Way to EMU", *Essays in International Finance*, No.187, June, 1992, Princeton University, New Jersey.
Frenkel J.A. & Goldstein M., *Key Issues in the Functioning of the International Monetary System: The Macroeconomic Implications of Currency Zones*, Paper Presented for the Economic Society of Australia and New Zealand, Sydney, Australia, October 18, 1991.
Frieden J.A., "Invested Interests: The Politics of National Economic Policies in a World of Global Finance", *International Organisation*, Vol.45, No.4, 1991.
Funabashi Y. (1988), *Managing the Dollar: From the Plaza to the Louvre*, Institute for International Economics, Washington.
Galbraith J.K. (1981), *The Crash of 1929*, Penguin, London.
Galtung J. (1973), *The European Community: A Superpower in the Making*, Allen & Unwin, Ltd., London.
Garrett G., "International Co-operation and Institutional Choice: The European Community's Internal Market", *International Organization*, Vol.46, No.2, Spring, 1992.
George S. (1991), *Politics and Policy in the European Community*, Oxford University Press, New York.

Gilpin R. "Three Models of the Future", in Modelski, ed., 1979.

_____ (1975), *US Power and the Multinational Corporation*, MacMillan & Co, Ltd., London.

Giovannini A. "The Transition to European Monetary Union", *Essays in International Finance*, No.178, November, 1990, Princeton University, New Jersey.

Giovannini A. & Spaventa L., "Fiscal Rules in the EMU: A 'No Entry Clause'", in Atkinson & Brunetta, ed., 1991.

Giovazzi F., Micossi S. & Miller M., ed., (1988), *The European Monetary System*, Cambridge University Press, London.

Goodhardt G., in Masson & Taylor, ed., 1993.

Gordon D.M., "The Global Economy: A New Edifice or Crumbling Foundation?", *New Left Review*, No.168, 1988.

Grahl J. & Teague P., "The Cost of Neo-Liberal Europe", *New Left Review*, No.174, 1989.

Guerrieri P. & Padoan P.C., "Neo-Mercantilism and International Economic Stability", *International Organization*, Vol.40, No.1, 1986.

_____ ed., (1989) *The Political Economy of European Integration*, Simon & Schuster, London.

Halevi J., "The EMS and the Bundesbank in Europe", in Arestis P. & Chick V., 1995.

Hall P.A., Patterns of Economic Policy: An Organizational Approach", in Bornstein et al, 1984.

Hallstein W. (1972), *Europe in the Making*, Allen & Unwin, Ltd., London.

Harrop J. (1989), *The Political Economy of Integration in the Community*, Edward Elgar Publishers, London.

Henderson W.O. (1962), *The Genesis of the Common Market*, Frank Cass & Co., Ltd., London.

Hine R.C. (1985), *The Political Economy of European Trade*, Wheatsheaf Books, Ltd., London.

Hodges M., ed., (1982), *European Integration*, Penguin Books, London.

Holland S., ed., (1983), *Out of Crisis: A Project for European Recovery*, Russell Press, London.

_____ (1975), *The Socialist Challenge*, Quartet Books, London.

_____ (1980), *UnCommon Market*, MacMillan & Co., London.

Hu Y.S. (1973), *The Impact of US Investment in Europe: A Case Study of the Automobile and Computer Industries*, Praeger Publishers, New York.

Humbert M., ed., (1993), *The Impact of Globalisation on Europe's Firms and Industries*, Pinter Publishers, London.

Ikenberry G.J., "A World Economy Restored: Expert Consensus and the Anglo-American Post-War Settlement", *International Organisation*, Vol.46, No.1, 1992.

Ingram J.C., "The Case for European Monetary Integration", *Essays in International Finance*, No.98, April, 1973, Princeton University, New Jersey.

Jacquemin A. & Sapir A., ed., (1989), *The European Internal Market*, Oxford University Press, New York.

Jenkins R., "European Monetary Union", *Loyds Bank Review*, January, 1978.

Johnson H.G. & Swoboda A.K., ed., (1973), *The Economics of Common Currencies*, Allen & Unwin, Ltd., London.

Josling T., "Agricultural Policies and World Trade", in Tsoukalis, ed., 1986.

Kaldor M. (1978), *The Disintegrating West*, Allen Lane, London.

Kalecki M. (1971), *Selected Essays on the Dynamics of the Capitalist Economy; 1933-70*, Cambridge University Press, London.

_____ (1954), *The Theory of Economic Dynamics*, Allen & Unwin, Ltd., London.

Keohane K.O., *After Hegemony*, Princeton University Press, USA.

Keynes J.M. (1920), *The Economic Consequences of the Peace*, MacMillan & Co., Ltd., London.

Kindleberger C.P. (1984), *A Financial History of Western Europe*, Allen & Unwin, London.

_____ "Germany's Persistent Balance of Payments Disequilibrium Revisited", *Banca Nazionale Del Lavoro*, June, 1976.

Kitzinger U.W. (1961), *The Challenge of the Common Market*, Basil Blackwell, Oxford.

Kolko J. & G. (1972), *The Limits of Power: The World and US Foreign Policy; 1945-54*, Harper & Row, New York.

Krause L.B. (1964), *The Common Market*, Prentice Hall, New York.

Krause L.B. & Salant W.S., ed., (1973), *European Monetary Unification and its Meaning for the US*, The Brookings Institution, Washington.

Krauss M.B., ed., (1973), *The Economics of Integration*, Allen & Unwin, Ltd., London.

Kriele M., "West Germany: The Dynamics of Expansion", *International Organization*, No.31, 1977.

Kriesler P., ed., (1993), *Australia and European Relations After Maastricht*, Centre for Applied Economic Research, Paper No. 28, University of New South Wales, Sydney, Australia.

Kruse D.C. (1980), *Monetary Integration in Western Europe: EMU, EMS and Beyond*, Butterworths, USA.

Lee R. & Ogden P.E., ed., (1976), *Economy and Society in the EEC*, Saxon House, London.

Lichtheim G. (1963), *Europe and America*, Thames & Hudson, London.

Lieberman S. (1977), *The Growth of European Mixed Economies: 1945-70*, Schenkman Publishers & Co., Inc., USA.

Lindberg L.N. (1963), *The Political Dynamics of European Integration*, Stanford University Press, USA.

Lindberg L.N. & Scheingold S.A. (1970), *Europe's Would-Be Polity*, Prentice-Hall, Inc., New Jersey.

Lipgens W. (1982), *A History of European Integration, Vol.1, 1945-47*, Oxford University Press, New York.

Llewellyn J. & Potter S., "Competitiveness and the Current Account", in Boltho, ed., 1982.

Lodge J., ed., (1983), *Institutions and Policy of the European Community*, Francis Pinter, London.

Mackler H., Martinelli A. & Smelser N., ed., *The New International Economy*, Sage Publishers, Inc., London.

Magnifico G., "European Monetary Unification For Balanced Growth: A New Approach", *Essays in International Finance*, August, 1971, Princeton University Press, New Jersey.

Maier C.S. (1987), *In Search of Stability*, Cambridge University Press, New York.

Mandel E. (1970), *Europe Vs America*, New Left Books, London.

_____ "The Laws of Uneven Development", *New Left Review*, No.59, 1970.

Masera R.S., "An Increasing Role for the ECU: A Character in Search of a Script", *Essays in International Finance*, No.167, June 1987, Princeton University, New jersey.

_____ "Europe's Economic Problems in an International Perspective", *Banca Nazionale Del Lavoro*, December, 1981.

_____ "The First Two Years of the EMS: The Exchange Rate Experience", *Banca Nazionale Del Lavoro*, September, 1981.

Masera R.S. & Triffin R., ed., (1984), *Europe's Money*, Clarendon Press, Oxford.

Masson P.R. & Taylor M.P. (1993), *Policy Issues in the Operation of Currency Unions*, Cambridge University Press, New York.

Mayer M. (1974), *The Bankers*, Weybridge & Tulley, New York.

Mayne R. & Pinter J. (1990), *Federal Union: The Pioneers*, MacMillan Press, London.

McEachern D. (1990), *The Expanding State: Class and Economy in Europe Since 1945*, St. Martins Press, New York.

McKinnon R.I., "Optimum Currency Areas", *American Economic Review*, No.53, 1963.

Meade J.E. (1955), *The Theory of Customs Unions*, North-Holland Publishing Company, Amsterdam.

Micossi S., "The Intervention and Financing Mechanisms of the EMS and the Role of the ECU", *Banca Nazionale Del Lavoro*, December, 1985.

Milward A.S. (1992), *The European Rescue of the Nation-State*, Routledge, London.

_____ (1984), *The Reconstruction of Western Europe:1945-51*, Methuen & Co., Ltd., London.

Modelski G., ed., (1979), *Transnational Corporations and World Order*, W.H. Freeman & Co., USA.

Molle W. & Cappellin R., ed., (1985), *Regional Impact of Community Policies in Europe*, Avery Publishers, UK.

Moon B.E., "Exchange Rate System, Policy Distortions and the Maintenance of Trade Dependence", *International Organization*, Vol.36, No.4, 1982.

Moravcsik A., "Negotiating the Single European Act: National Interests and Conventional Statecraft in the EC", *International Organization*, Vol.45, No.1, 1991.

Mundel R.A., "A Theory of Optimum Currency Areas", *American Economic Review*, No.51, 1961.

Myrdal G. (1957), *Economic Theory and Underdeveloped Regions*, Gerald Duckworth & Co., Ltd., London.

Nairn T., "British Nationalism and the EEC", *New Left Review*, No.69, 1971.

_____ (1973), *The Left Against Europe*, Penguin Books, London.

Naudin T., "We Need Monetary Union More Than Ever", *The European*, 17-23 March, 1995.

_____ "Guardian of Single Currency prepares to go into Battle", *The European*, 16-22 June, 1995.

Nugent N. (1991), *The Government and Politics of the European Community*, MacMillan & Co., London.

OECD, "Implementation of the Euro: Key Considerations from the International Business Perspective", 5/11/97, Paris.

Owen N. (1983), *Economies of Scale, Competitiveness and Trade Patterns Within the European Community*, Clarendon Press, Oxford.

Padoa-Schioppa T., ed., (1987), *Efficiency, Stability and Equity,* Oxford University Press, New York.

_____ "Europe After 1992: Three Essays", *Essays in International Finance,* No.182, May 1991, Princeton University, New Jersey.

_____ , in Giovazzi et al., ed., 1988.

_____ ed., (1984), *Money, Economic Policy and Europe,* Commission of the EC, Brussels.

Papadantonokis K., in Arrighi, ed., 1985.

Parboni R. (1981), *The Dollar and Its Rivals,* New Left Books, London.

_____ "The Dollar Weapon: From Nixon to Reagan", *New Left Review,* No.158, 1986.

_____ "Reflections on Williamsburg", *New Left Review,* No.141, 1983.

Pelkmans J. & Winters A. (1988), *Europe's Domestic Market,* Routledge, London.

Petit P., "Expansionary Policies in a Restrictive World: The Case of France", in Guerrieri, et al., 1989.

Pinder J. (1991), *European Community,* Oxford University Press, New York.

_____ ed., (1982), *National Industrial Strategies and the World Economy,* Allanheld, Osmun & Co., USA.

_____ (1991), *The European Community and Eastern Europe,* Royal Institute of International Affairs, London.

Pinder J. & Pryce R. (1969), *Europe After De Gaulle,* Penguin Books, London.

Pollard S. (1974), *European Economic Integration: 1815-1970,* Thames & Hudson, Ltd., London.

Pomfret R. (1986), *Mediterranean Policy of the Eurpean Community,* MacMillan Press, Ltd., London.

Postan M.M. (1967), *An Economic History of Western Europe: 1945-64,* Methuen & Co., Ltd., London.

Poulantzas N., "Internationalisation of Capitalist Relations and the Nation-State", *Economy & Society,* Vol. 3, No.2, 1974.

Pryce R. (1973), *The Politics of the European Community,* Butterworth, UK.

Radice H., ed., (1975), *International Firms and Modern Imperialism,* Penguin Books, London.

Richardson H., "EC-Japan Relations - After Adolescence", *Nissan Occasional Paper,* No.12, 1989.

Robson P. (1980), *The Economics of International Integration,* Allen & Unwin, London.

Rowthorn B., "Imperialism in the Seventies - Unity or Rivalry?", in Radice, ed., 1975.

Ross G., "Confronting the New Europe", *New Left Review*, No.191, 1992.

Salvati M., "May 1968 and the Hot Autumn of 1969: The Responses of Two Ruling Classes", in Berger S., ed., 1981.

Sandholtz W., "Choosing Union: Monetary Politics and Maastricht", *International Organization*, Vol.47, No.1, Winter, 1993.

Sarcinelli M., "The EMS and the International Monetary system: Towards Greater Stabilility", *Banca Nazionale Del Lavoro*, March, 1986.

Scaperlanda A.E. & Mauer L.J., "The Determinants of US Direct Investment in the EEC" *American Economic Review*, Vol.59, No.3, September, 1969.

Schumpeter J.A. (1939), *Business Cycles, Vol 1 & 2*, MacGraw-Hill, New York.

Seers D. & Ostrom K., ed., (1983), *The Crisis of the European Regions*, MacMillan Press, London.

Seers D. & Vaitsos C., ed., (1980), *Integration & Unequal Development: The Experience of the EEC*, MacMillan Press, London.

Senghaas D. (1985), *The European Experience: A Historical Critique of Development Theory*, Berg Publishers, Ltd., New Hampshire, USA.

Servan-Schreiber J.J. (1969), *The American Challenge*, Atheneum, New York.

Shanks M. (1977), *European Social Policy, Today and Tomorrow*, Pergamon Press, Ltd., London.

Shoup L.H. & Minter W. (1977), *Imperial Brain Trust: The Council on Foreign Relations and US Foreign Policy*, Monthly Review Press, New York.

Skitovsky T. (1958), *Economic Theory and Western European Integration*, Allen & Unwin, London.

Smaghi L.B., "Progressing Towards European Monetary Integration: Selected Issues and Proposals", *Temi Di Discussione Del Servizio Studi*, No.187, January, 1993, Banca D'Italia.

Spaulding R.M., "German Trade Policy in Eastern Europe, 1890-1990: Preconditions for Applying Trade Leverage", *International Organization*, Vol.45, No.3, 1991.

Spero J.E. (1977), *The Politics of International Economic Relations*, St. Martins Press, Inc., London.

Spinelli A. (1966), *The Eurocrats*, John Hopkins Press, USA.

_____ "The Growth of the European Movement Since the Second World War", in Hodges, ed., 1972.

Stanners W., "Is Inflation an Important Condition for High Growth?", *Cambridge Journal of Economics*, No.17, 1993.

Sternberg F. (1947), *The Coming Crisis*, Richard Clay, London.

Strauss E. (1958), *Common Sense About the Common Market*, Allen & Unwin, London.

Svennilson I. (1954), *Growth and Stagnation in the European Economy*, United Nations Economic Commission for Europe, Geneva.

Swann D. (1983), *Competition and Industrial Policy in the European Community*, Metheun, New York.

_____ ed., (1978), *The Economics of the Common Market*, Penguin Books, London.

Sylos-Labini P. (1969), *Oligopoly and Technical Progress*, Harvard University Press, USA.

Taber G.M. (1974), *Patterns and Prospects of Common Market Trade*, Peter Owen, Ltd., London.

Tanzer M. (1980), *The Energy Crisis*, Monthly Review Press, New York.

Tavlas G.S., "On the International Use of Currencies: The Case of the Deutsche Mark", *Essays in International Finance*, No.181, March, 1991, Princeton University, New Jersey.

Tew B. (1960), *International Monetary Co-operation*, Hutchinson & Co., Ltd., London.

The Economist, "Business in Europe", June 8, 1991.

_____ "EMU Survey", June 11, 1998.

_____ "Europe Falls to Earth" August 7, 1993.

_____ "Europe's Internal Market", July 9, 1988.

_____ "The All Saint's Day Manifesto For EMU", November 1, 1975.

_____ "The Battle for Europe", June 3, 1991.

Thirwall A., "The Balance of Payments Constraint as an Explanation for International Growth Differences", *Banca Nazionale Del Lavoro*, Vol.32, No.128, March, 1979.

Thurow L. (1992), *Head to Head*, Allen & Unwin, Pty., Ltd., New York.

Thygessen N., "Are Monetary Policies and Performances Converging?", *Banca Nazionale Del Lavoro*, September, 1981.

Triffin R., "Europe and the Money Muddle Revisited", *Banca Nazionale Del Lavoro*, March, 1978.

_____ (1961), *Gold and the Dollar Crisis*, Yale University Press, New York.

_____ "The IMS (International Monetary System....or Scandal) and the EMS", *Banca Nazionale Del Lavoro*, September, 1987.

Tsoukalis L., ed., (1986), *Europe, America and the World Economy*, Basil Blackwell, Oxford.

_____ (1993), *The New European Economy*, Oxford University Press, New York.

_____ ed., (1985), *The Political Economy of International Money*, Sage Publishers, Ltd., London.

_____ (1977), *The Politics and Economics of European Monetary Integration*, Allen & Unwin, Ltd., London.

Tugendhat C. (1986), *Making Sense of Europe*, Viking Press, UK.

_____ (1971), *The Multinationals*, Penguin Books, London.

Vaitsos C., in Seers & Vaitsos, ed., 1980.

Vanhove N. & Klaasen L.H., (1980), ed., *Regional Policy: A European Approach*, Saxon House, UK.

Van Ypersele J. & Koeune J.C. (1984), *The European Monetary System*, Commission of the EC, Brussels.

Varga E. (1963), *Twentieth Century Capitalism*, Lawrence & Wishart, London.

Vernon R., "International Investment and International Trade in the Product Cycle", *Quarterly Journal of Economics*, May, 1966.

_____ (1971), *Sovereignty at Bay*, Basic Books, USA.

Viner J. (1950), *The Customs Union Issue*, Stevens & Sons, Ltd., London.

Wallace W. (1990), *The Transformation of Western Europe*, Pinter Publishers, London.

Wallerstein I. (1979), *The Capitalist World Economy*, Cambridge University Press, London.

Weissburg R., "Nationalism, Integration and French and German Elites", *International Organization*, Vol. 23, 1969.

Willis F.R. (1968), *France, Germany and the New Europe; 1945-67*, Stanford University Press, USA.

_____ (1971), *Italy Chooses Europe*, Oxford University Press, London.

Winters L.A. & Venables A.J., (1991), ed., *European Integration: Trade & Industry*, Cambridge University Press, London.

Wistrich E. (1989), *After 1992: The United States of Europe*, Routledge, London.

Woolcock S., Hodges M. & Schreiber K. (1991), *Britain, Germany & 1992*, The Royal Institute of International Affairs, Pinter Publishers, London.

Yondorf W., "Monnet and the Action Committee", *International Organization*, Vol.19, 1965.

For Product Safety Concerns and Information please contact our EU
representative GPSR@taylorandfrancis.com Taylor & Francis Verlag GmbH,
Kaufingerstraße 24, 80331 München, Germany

Printed and bound by CPI Group (UK) Ltd, Croydon, CR0 4YY
08/05/2025
01864366-0006